MERE
CHRISTIANS

JORDAN RAYNOR AND KALEIGH COX

HARVEST HOUSE PUBLISHERS
EUGENE, OREGON

TO THE TRUE AUTHOR

OF THESE AND ALL

OUR FAVORITE STORIES

Published in association with the literary agency of Legacy, LLC.

Illustrations by Ken Jacobsen.
Cover design by Faceout Studio, Amanda Hudson. Interior design by Aesthetic Soup, Jeff Jansen.
Photo of Jordan Raynor by Kari Bellamy. Photo of Kaleigh Cox by Maggie McGaugh.

For bulk, special sales, or ministry purchases, please call 1-800-547-8979.
Email: CustomerService@hhpbooks.com

FIVE MERE CHRISTIANS

Copyright © 2025 by Jordan Raynor
Published by Harvest House Publishers
Eugene, Oregon 97408
www.harvesthousepublishers.com

ISBN 978-0-7369-9170-4 (hardcover)
ISBN 978-0-7369-9171-1 (eBook)

Library of Congress Control Number: 2024950192

Printed in Colombia

25 26 27 28 29 30 31 32 33 / NI / 10 9 8 7 6 5 4 3 2 1

CONTENTS

INTRODUCTION

You're not a pastor, missionary, or religious professional. You're a mere Christian like me (Jordan) who works as an entrepreneur, teacher, or mechanic. And you *deeply* want to glorify God in every aspect of your life—including your work.

But what on earth does that look like *practically*?

How do you embrace your role in the "royal priesthood" (1 Peter 2:9) when you spend more time preparing PowerPoint presentations than you do praying prayers? How can you be "salt and light" (Matthew 5:13-16) in a dark industry without losing your job *or* your saltiness? How do you work at a pace that allows you to "serve" your clients or employer "wholeheartedly" (Ephesians 6:7) while being unhurried enough to experience and extend God's love throughout your day?

These questions are where the rubber meets the proverbial road, and there are two ways to answer them. I could *tell* you the answers through theological exposition. Or I could *show* you through stories. There is a place for the former. But this book gives you the latter.

LESS TELLING, MORE SHOWING

Pastor Tim Keller once said, "You never learn anything spiritually valuable by being told. You have to be shown."[1]

I think that's part of the reason "the Word became flesh" (John 1:14). Because while God knew that you and I needed to be *told* how to glorify him through his living written Word, he also knew that we needed to be *shown* how to glorify him through the lived Word of Jesus Christ. I think God knew that we humans need flesh-and-bone, three-dimensional models to understand what it looks like practically to glorify him.

Of course, we have the perfect model in Jesus Christ. But we *also* have imperfect yet helpful models of how to glorify God in Jesus's followers. This is why the apostle Paul said, "Follow my example, as I follow the example of Christ" (1 Corinthians 11:1).

Paul understood that he had a unique story that would make the idea of following Jesus more concrete to those who shared his work, stage of life, and cultural context. And so he encouraged those believers to look to him as an animated case study on how to glorify God.

Paul's words point to an important principle: If you want to know what it looks like practically to glorify God, look first to Christ and second to Christ's followers. And that is exactly what this book is designed to help you do.

In the following pages, I'll introduce you to five mere Christians whose examples you and I would be wise to follow because of how well they followed the example of Christ—five men and women who will show you how to practically glorify God in your work.

Fred Rogers—the creator of *Mister Rogers' Neighborhood*—will show you how to glorify God by treating your current job as a "priestly" duty, making time to truly experience the love of God while you work, and living at a pace that allows you to extend that love to others you encounter Monday through Friday.

Fannie Lou Hamer—the civil rights activist who stood up to President Johnson on national TV—will show you how to glorify God by working for justice without hating the unjust, embracing the tension between trusting in God and hustling at work, and believing that God is creating an impact through your work even when that work appears to be in vain.

Ole Kirk Christiansen—the founder of LEGO—will show you how to glorify God by persevering through life's most brutal trials, embracing playful work the world calls "useless," and committing yourself to the highest standards of your craft.

Hannah More—the poet largely credited for abolishing slavery throughout the British Empire—will show you how to glorify God by refusing to isolate from "dark" places, working to change the world through culture and not just politics, and showing an uncommon audacity that can be explained only by a humble confidence in God.

C.S. Lewis—the author of *The Chronicles of Narnia* and *Mere Christianity*—will show you how to glorify God by finding your ultimate joy in Christ and not your work, treating everything at work as evangelism, not just your words, and embracing your role as a mere Christian as one of the Church's most effective means of making disciples of Jesus Christ.

The stories of these five mere Christians each stand on their own. So feel free to pick and choose which ones you will read. But before you crack open the first story, I want to make one thing clear…

THESE ARE NOT YOUR TYPICAL BIOGRAPHIES

If you're like me, you probably have a love-hate relationship with biographies. Which is why the stories in this book differ from traditional biographies in three significant ways.

1. They are mercifully short.

I'm interested in Winston Churchill. But I'm not interested enough to read the three-*thousand*-page tome that is hailed as the best biography on his life.

I want biographies I can finish in a single sitting, and I'm not interested in reading everything the person ever wrote. I just want the action—the juicy stuff—the most compelling, made-for-TV scenes from somebody's life that when put together, give me a relatively complete portrait of their life without having to zoom in on every brushstroke.

I'm betting you feel the same way. And that's what you will find in the five mercifully short biographies that make up this book, each of which can be read in under an hour.

2. They are extremely entertaining.

Most of C.S. Lewis's biographers agree that Lewis had an affair with his best friend's mom. Scandalous, right? And *super* interesting in light of Lewis's future redemption. But trust me: You would fall asleep reading about this affair in most Lewis biographies because rather than focusing on the story, they spend twenty pages summarizing every letter the alleged lovers ever wrote to each other.

You will *not* find that type of biography in this book. My cowriter Kaleigh Cox and I have set out to write a "can't put it down" version of these mere Christians' stories that are as entertaining as fiction but all entirely true—biographies that are as page-turning as James Patterson's novels and as helpful as Tim Keller's sermons. This brings me to the third and final thing that makes the biographies in this collection different.

3. They are profoundly helpful.

Unlike most biographies where the story is an end in and of itself, the biographies in this book are a means to an end—namely, showing you how to practically glorify God in your own work as a mere Christian today.

To that end, each biography in this book concludes with a section called "Three Ways to Glorify God in Your Work" to help you apply what you saw animated in each story. Although most biographies make their subjects out to be heroes we mortals could never dream of emulating, this collection intentionally does not.

Why? Because the same Holy Spirit that was at work in Rogers, Hamer, Christiansen, More, and Lewis is at work in you today, believer. And so, you and I can glorify God in the same ways these men and women did if we will hear and respond to their stories.

Are you ready to see what it looks like practically to be guided by that same Spirit to glorify God in your work? Good! Then let's begin.

PART I

FRED ROGERS

CREATOR OF *MISTER ROGERS' NEIGHBORHOOD*

HOW TO GLORIFY GOD BY EMBRACING YOUR CALLING,
EXPERIENCING YOUR BELOVEDNESS, AND ELIMINATING ALL HURRY

If neckties could tell tales, the one Fred Rogers is buried in would tell an epic one.

With a black-and-blue tartan pattern, it was the style traditionally worn by ordained Presbyterian ministers as they preached from the pulpit.

But Fred Rogers was no pastor. He was the host of *Mister Rogers' Neighborhood*, an educational children's show that ran on public television for over thirty years.

Each episode began in much the same way: A traffic light blinking yellow was a subtle reminder to slow down. And then Mr. Rogers himself would enter singing "It's a Beautiful Day in the Neighborhood" as he removed his suit jacket, zipped up his sweater, and changed his shoes. Throughout the familiar routine, he'd maintain a warm smile and eye contact with the camera.

After the song closed, Fred would talk to his young audience—directly and through puppets—and help them process topics ranging from anger and fear to divorce and death.

Each child watching would feel as if Mister Rogers was talking only to them. But across more than nine hundred episodes, Fred was connecting with millions of children. In the mid-1980s, when the show was at its peak, nearly 10 percent of American households tuned in on a regular basis.

By that point, the show seemed inevitable. But the truth is that *Mister Rogers' Neighborhood* almost never happened at all.

In 1955, just as his career in television was first taking off, Fred felt conflicted. He enjoyed his work as a writer and cohost of a program called *The Children's Corner*. He loved working with children and was a natural in front of the camera. But according to one biographer, "He couldn't quite give up the idea of service through the church he'd found attractive as a young boy sitting in the pews with his mother."[1]

And so he enrolled in Pittsburgh Theological Seminary, located across town from the television station where he worked.

Every weekday for eight years, he arrived at the station early to begin work. He stopped midday to drive thirty blocks to class and then returned to the studio for a live broadcast.

Despite the demands of both his career and his coursework, Fred Rogers excelled at both, graduating magna cum laude with a master of divinity in 1963.

But somewhere in the midst of all those drives back and forth between seminary and the studio, an idea began to form within him.

What if his career and calling weren't opposite trajectories after all? What if he was called not to choose but to combine? To carry the work of ministry onto a television set? To serve a congregation of young children behind puppets rather than pulpits?

The idea was radical. And the elders of the Pittsburgh Presbytery were not on board. They urged Fred to pursue a traditional path of ministry, preaching on Sundays in a church body and ministering to the congregation the rest of the week.

Perhaps "urged" is not the right word. They *commanded* it.

The local presbytery held the power of assignment, and Fred simply would not be assigned to a children's television program. It wasn't done.

But Fred couldn't let the idea go. Fortunately, Fred wasn't alone in his conviction that there is more to Christian ministry than giving sermons and pastoring a congregation. His friend Reverend Bill Barker was teaching part time at the seminary and decided to go before the elders to challenge their decision.

Barker argued on behalf of Fred: "Look, here's an individual who has his pulpit proudly in front of a TV camera. His congregation are little people from the ages of about two or three on up to about seven or eight. And this is a whole congregation of hundreds of thousands if not millions of kids, and this is a man who has been authentically called by the Lord as much as any of you guys sitting out there."[2]

Barker's plea was a success, and in June 1963, Fred was ordained in front of his family, friends, and fellow ministers. The day was sunny with a pleasant breeze, the service was full of Fred's favorite music, and everyone involved seemed caught up in the joy of this unusual ordination service.

It was Barker who did the honors of formally charging Fred with his official role in ministry: "We charge you to shake us through a God who involves

Himself in our world, into the world where He already is…This world of TV cameras, of puppets, of children, of parents, of studios, of directors, of actors, this [too] is God's world…We, as the Church, charge that you speak to us to disturb us…We charge you to speak to us to remind us that we too, through you, must be involved."[3]

Not long after that service, Barker went on a trip to Scotland and returned with a gift for his newly ordained friend: a black-and-blue, tartan-patterned tie, which a delighted Fred declared his "clergy tie."

"I like to wear this on [*Neighborhood*] to give a subliminal message," Fred once shared with a conspiratorial smile.[4] He eventually chose to be buried in the tie—but not until he'd lived a lot of life in it first.

Few people know that the calm, steady Fred Rogers threw away his dream show not once but twice, and with no real plan for what was next. Or that *Mister Rogers' Neighborhood* would have been canceled before it even really began if not for the protests of thousands of superfan moms. Or that he was so disciplined he weighed in at precisely 143 pounds every single day of his adult life—yet so whimsical he didn't hesitate to throw his head back and laugh at the pranks Michael Keaton orchestrated on set.

The life of Fred Rogers is full of both delightful surprises and invaluable lessons. It's a story of how all Christians—not just pastors and religious professionals—can glorify God in their work. It's a case study of what it looks like to work at the pace of Jesus and experience the love of God amid the busyness of daily life. But above all, it's a story of how pouring your life out in service of others can offer glimpses of heaven on earth.

CHAPTER 2

The kidnapping was called the biggest story "since the Resurrection."[5] But when the body of famous aviator Charles Lindbergh's one-year-old son was found partly buried within five miles of the family home, it was a trial, not a miracle, that followed.

The whole world had watched with bated breath as the frantic family responded to ransom notes via newspaper headlines. So, even after the kidnapper was arrested, wealthy parents like Jim and Nancy Rogers worried their children would be the next target.

There was, after all, a considerable fortune that could be squeezed from the Rogers family. Nancy, whose family had the foresight to be early investors in radio, had brought a sizable inheritance into her marriage.

Everyone in the small working-class town of Latrobe, Pennsylvania, knew the beautiful young couple and celebrated with them when Fred McFeely Rogers was born on March 20, 1928. Their three-story brick home had plenty of room for a growing family, but after a long and difficult labor, Nancy was grieved to hear doctors advise that her first birth also be her last.

Still, the tight-knit community of Latrobe was the perfect place to raise a son. Its welcoming, tree-lined streets and picturesque homes would eventually form the inspiration for the model town that appears in every episode of *Mister Rogers' Neighborhood*. And yet, after the Lindbergh family's worst nightmare played out in the headlines, not even Latrobe felt safe anymore.

Jim and Nancy held their only son closely and ensured he was under constant supervision. When it was time for Fred to start school, he didn't ride the bus or walk to class with other children but instead rode in a limousine under the watchful eye of the family's private driver.

Of course, no matter how much money you have or how many people you employ, it's impossible to protect your child forever. One day, when school let out earlier than expected, Fred didn't see anyone waiting for him in front of Latrobe Elementary School and began to walk the ten blocks home.

Despite his parents' fears, there were no greedy kidnappers lurking in the shadows. But when you're a shy, overweight young boy often bedridden due to a bad case of asthma, that's not why you're looking over your shoulder anyway.

"It wasn't long before I sensed I was being followed—by a whole group of boys," Fred later recalled. "As I walked faster, I looked around. They called my name and came closer and closer and got louder and louder."[6]

"Freddy! Hey, fat Freddy! We're going to get you, Freddy!"

Their taunts mingled with the pounding sounds of their footsteps and his own rapidly beating heart as he broke into a run.

As he ran, Fred prayed for refuge. *Lord, please let Mrs. Stewart be home, please let Mrs. Stewart be home.* When he fell against her door, panting and knocking, his prayers were answered. The door swung open, and he stepped inside, shaking but safe at last.

The family's driver arrived to pick Fred up a little while later, and it was a changed boy who slid into the limo's back seat. He had, for the first time, felt the tangible, personal love of God for him. It would stick with him for the rest of his life.

Years later, Fred recalled, "The tough times I've been through…turned out to be times in which God's presence was so clear—so real that it felt like Mrs. Stewart opening her door and taking me into her safe home."[7]

But if the moment of rescue changed young Fred, so did the chase itself. "I resented the teasing. I resented the pain. I resented those kids for not seeing beyond my fatness or my shyness," he later shared.[8]

As he processed that resentment, his vulnerable sensitivity took on a new shape. It became empathetic compassion, a trait for which he'd eventually become known the world over.

"[After that day,] I sought out stories of other people who were poor in spirit, and I felt for them," remembered Fred. "I started to look behind the things that people did and said and…after a lot of sadness, I began a lifelong search for what is essential, what it is about my neighbor that doesn't meet the eye."[9]

With this new perspective, Fred began paying closer attention to how his parents moved through a hurting world. In the comfort afforded by wealth,

Jim and Nancy Rogers could have turned a blind eye to the less fortunate and embraced a life of leisure. But they did nothing of the sort.

When Jim walked the floor at his numerous factories around town, it was with a sharp eye for opportunities—not to correct but to connect. He'd ask employees about their lives and families, listening carefully and making mental notes of those in need.

Then, when he got home, he'd report what he'd learned to Nancy, who always sprang into action. Mrs. Rogers organized and led a volunteer ministry composed of several local churches dedicated to meeting needs in the community. Jim and Nancy Rogers, who took seriously God's command to do justice, love mercy, and walk humbly, often used their own money to buy what was needed.

Nearly everyone in town had been a beneficiary of the couple's generosity, or at least knew someone who was. After a while, "the school nurse at Latrobe Elementary School would just order shoes, coats, eyeglasses, and even furniture and have the bills sent directly to Nancy Rogers."[10]

Each year, Nancy began Christmas shopping in June, buying around 1,500 gifts that she picked out—or knitted—herself.

Her husband had his own methods of radical generosity. When he died, his personal ledger book held the records of thousands of loans he'd quietly given to employees with apparently no effort at collection.

As Fred grew from a young, shy "fat Freddy" to a more thoughtful teenager, he became increasingly convinced of his parents' belief that life is for service. And as he sat by their side in the pews of Latrobe Presbyterian Church on Sunday mornings, he wondered whether a role in ministry might be how he served the world.

But as he was about to discover, committing to his "why" came easily. Discerning his "how" would be much harder.

CHAPTER 3

His dorm was like a scene from *Animal House*, and Fred Rogers could not have felt more out of place.

It would be another decade before Chris Miller, the scriptwriter who based that movie on his own experiences at Dartmouth College, arrived on campus, but the school's party culture was already alive and well when Fred enrolled as a freshman.

Dartmouth was still a men-only school, and Fred's roommates were rowdy football players who partied every weekend. Eventually, Fred became so uncomfortable with their antics that he moved in with his French teacher to escape the wild dormitory.

He'd arrived at Dartmouth in 1946, just as World War II came to an end, full of hope and excitement about all the possibilities ahead. After the teasing he'd endured in childhood, Fred had finally found his place in high school as a serious, confident scholar.

One of his high school classmates, legendary golfer Arnold Palmer, recalled, "[Fred] was a very meticulous student. He didn't run with the guys like I did, and he didn't drink beer. I did. We all did…His interests were music and religion and history and that sort of thing. But a nice guy. We liked each other."[11]

Fred was well liked, or at least well respected, by many at Latrobe High School. His peers voted him student council president and most likely to succeed, and he graduated salutatorian of his class. His girlfriend stood beside him at graduation as class valedictorian.

After finding his footing in high school, he was frustrated to find himself back on shaky social ground at Dartmouth. The quiet, studious Fred turned to music to cope with the isolation—a lifelong habit that was developing into a real passion.

After two years, Fred approached a favorite professor with an idea. He wanted to change his major from Romance languages to music—but Dartmouth did not yet have a developed music department. The professor, who had recently come to Dartmouth from Rollins College in Florida, recommended Fred check out their program instead.

From the moment his plane touched down at the airport in Florida to visit Rollins, Fred's experience diverged drastically from the loneliness he'd endured in his freshman and sophomore years at Dartmouth. A group of young music majors were waiting to greet him with warm smiles and a tour of the school. Among them was Joanne Byrd, Fred's future wife.

"We piled into the antique Franklin that had lots of room. We were hanging out the windows of the car when he came out," recalled Joanne years later. "We grabbed him, and took him right with us, and made him one of us. He blended in so well."[12]

Transferring from an Ivy League school to a smaller, little-known college in Winter Park, Florida, would be, by the world's standards, a step down. But Fred sensed that for him, this was a step in the right direction.

Surrounded by new friends, Fred continued to take his work seriously but also felt the freedom to relax. One friend and classmate recalled that whenever Fred would pass a marble plaque on campus engraved with the phrase "Life Is for Service," he would flash a mischievous smile and cover "ser" so that it would read "Life Is for vice" instead.

While the sign provided Fred with an opportunity to evoke grins from his friends, it was also a constant reminder of his vision for his own life. He would eventually hang a photo of that sign in his office, a continued daily reminder that "life is for service" even as that life took him far beyond the Rollins campus.

But well into his four years of undergraduate studies, that future was still unclear. Fred was at a loss for how exactly he would serve God and others through his career.

In high school, he'd considered becoming a Presbyterian minister or an airline pilot. In college, Fred "drove his parents crazy, because every year he had a different idea about what he was going to do. He was going to be a diplomat, then he was going to be a French teacher, then he was going to run an orphanage, then he was going to be a musician."[13]

While the constant changing of plans may have seemed chaotic to his parents, Fred was patiently exploring all his options. Years later, when enrolled in seminary, he would meet Professor Bill Orr, a mentor who would give Fred the words that explained his approach to vocation. He called it a "guided drift."

What may have seemed like aimless drifting to others was actually guided by the Holy Spirit and Fred's longstanding commitment to living a life of service.

"The drift was allowing oneself the creative freedom to follow not just your interests, but where life would lead you…allowing the opportunities that come along to spark your creativity and allowing yourself the freedom to go after them," explained Fred's biographer Max King. "Yet everything was based on his strong [Christian] values and his strong commitment to excellence."[14]

Jim Rogers held out hope that his son would "drift" right back to Latrobe to work alongside him in the family's businesses. But as Fred's college graduation date drew near, he seemed to have finally made up his mind. He was accepted to Western Theological Seminary, where he could pursue his childhood dream of becoming a Presbyterian minister.

But then, during a visit home over Easter break during his senior year, Fred discovered something in his parents' living room that would shock him and change the course of his life forever.

CHAPTER 4

You know, I don't think I'll go into seminary right away."

With graduation just nine weeks away, Fred was reporting yet another change of heart to his parents. "I think maybe I'll go into television," he said.[15]

It was quite an announcement coming from someone who had just that week seen a television for the first time. Jim and Nancy Rogers had only recently purchased one of the first TV sets in town.

"I went home my senior year for a vacation in Latrobe, and I saw this new thing called television," Fred would later recall. "And I saw people dressed in some kind of costumes, literally throwing pies in each other's faces."

The cheap attempt at humor "astounded" Fred, who found the behavior degrading and inappropriate for young viewers. "This could be a wonderful tool for education. Why is it being used this way?" he wondered.[16]

His decision to pivot into television may have been abrupt, but it wasn't random. In fact, it was the culmination of many interests—particularly in education and music.

But it would be over a decade before Fred came to understand that he'd stumbled upon his calling in his parents' living room that day.

"I'll never forget the sense of wholeness I felt when I finally realized what I was—songwriter, telecommunicator, student of human development, language buff—but that all those things and more could be used in the service of children's healthy growing," he'd later explain to a group of new college graduates.

"The directions weren't written in invisible ink on the back of my diploma. They came ever so slowly for me; and ever so firmly I trusted that they would emerge. All I can say is, it's worth the struggle to discover who you really are."[17]

Fred's willingness to consider a wide variety of career paths as opportunities to serve God and others was remarkable—and his parents' support of that exploration even more so.

Not far from Latrobe, future actor Jimmy Stewart was also growing up in a Christian household. He had a "tough, demanding father" whose "sense of Presbyterian propriety led him to relentlessly pressure Jimmy to leave the profession of acting, which he did not consider a proper, Christian calling."[18]

Jim Rogers, on the other hand, gave Fred his full support. Even though he didn't fully understand his son's vision, he used his connections to help Fred land his first job after graduation: an entry-level position at NBC.

As an assistant, Fred's job was to fetch "coffee and Cokes" for people who often ignored or dismissed him. In an interview years later, Fred endeared himself to anyone who's ever had a bad internship when he recalled a time "he brought coffee to someone…who took one sip and said curtly, 'I wanted milk and not sugar.'"[19]

But as he took drink orders and ran errands, Fred was also watching the pioneers of modern television shape the future of the entertainment industry. His bosses included Sylvester "Pat" Weaver, creator of *The Today Show*, and Kirk Browning, whose many accolades included four Emmy Awards and a Peabody Award.

With a foot in the door at NBC, Fred's career path was full of possibility. His personal life, on the other hand, remained a bit hazy—particularly where Joanne Byrd was concerned.

After developing a close friendship in college, Fred and Joanne had kept in touch beyond graduation. But with a thousand miles between them—Joanne was in graduate school at Florida State—both were casually seeing other people.

And then Fred's parents intervened.

It was on Jim and Nancy Rogers's annual winter vacation to Florida that Joanne stopped by for a visit with her friend Cristophe in tow. Although warm and friendly, Mr. and Mrs. Rogers kept a sharp eye on the pair. And once the visit was over, they wasted no time in giving Fred a call.

Whatever they said or did is a mystery, but it seems to have served as a moment of epiphany for Fred. A few days later, he wrote to Joanne, asking for her hand in marriage. And then he waited—until, at last, the phone rang at his apartment.

"Hello?" Fred answered. After a brief but loaded pause, he heard one word from the other end: "Sh*t."

Joanne, full of nerves, had blanked on what to say and blurted out the word of graffiti she'd been staring at in the phone booth. The two shared a nervous laugh before Joanne finally found the word she'd been looking for: "Yes."

After an elegant wedding on June 9, 1952, and a honeymoon in Europe, the newlyweds made their home in New York, where Fred was quickly climbing the ladder at NBC. Higher-ups at the network were even considering him as a potential host of an upcoming variety show when another call from his parents changed the course of his life once again.

Pittsburgh was launching a new TV station called WQED, Jim told Fred. Wouldn't he like to move home and be on the ground floor of the network?

When his mentor and friends at NBC learned Fred was taking his father's suggestion seriously, they were shocked. "They said, 'You are nuts. That place isn't even on the air yet, and you're in line to be a producer or a director or anything you want to be here,'" Fred later recalled.[20]

But to Fred, the opportunity to pivot into educational television felt like "the right place at the very right time…It gave me a chance to use all the talents that I had ever been given."[21] At WQED, he hoped he might even have the freedom to shape a program of his own.

"I'd love to have guests and present a whole smorgasbord of ways for the children to choose," he'd say later, recounting his early idea for a show. "Some child might choose painting; some child might choose playing the cello. There are so many ways of saying who we are and how we feel. Ways that don't hurt anybody. And it seems to me that this is a great gift."[22]

But Fred wasn't quite done learning that having a vision is just the first step. Achieving it is another matter entirely.

CHAPTER 5

When Dorothy Daniel purchased a small tiger hand puppet in March 1954, she never could have imagined the cultural phenomenon she was setting into motion.

As the general manager of WQED, she was simply preparing for a celebratory staff dinner the night before the station's new show, *The Children's Corner*, was scheduled to go on air. She wanted to show her appreciation for the staff by placing a small, handpicked gift at each person's place at the table.

As she worked her way down the list, she came to Fred Rogers. She'd never seen him perform with puppets, but she'd heard he liked using them when engaging with children. So, when Fred arrived for dinner on March 31, he found a small tiger puppet waiting for him.

Delighted by the thoughtful gift, Fred named the little tiger after its giver. And the very next day, Daniel Striped Tiger made his debut on set. At the start of the show, he popped out of a hole in a clock with the time and a fact for the show's host: "Hi, Josie. It's 5:02, and Columbus discovered America in 1492!"

"That was the first thing that he said, and I had no idea that he'd say any more," Fred later recalled.[23]

But an hour a day was a lot of programming to fill, and the weekly budget of $150 for *The Children's Corner* barely covered salaries for the show's hosts, Fred Rogers and Josie Carey. Daniel Tiger was soon making regular appearances to chat with Josie and fill air time cheaply.

"When [Dorothy] Daniel asked who wants to do a children's program, Josie and I said, 'We'll do it for an hour a day,'" Fred would later explain. "Can you imagine producing an hour a day? I combed the country for free films we could put in...We had things like how to grow grass in New Hampshire. No one had any idea how hard it would be to fill an hour of programming a day."[24]

But even watching grass grow was, by Fred's estimation, a serious improvement upon the pie-in-the-face, slapstick humor so common to other children's programs. It was, after all, that appalling behavior that had inspired him to create something better in the first place.

But now that he had a platform, it wasn't entirely clear what that something better should be.

Eventually, Fred would be known for meticulously planning his programs, but in the early days of *The Children's Corner*, he and Josie would simply jot down some ideas on a single page from a yellow legal pad and then improvise on air.

Josie Carey was the host and face of the show, while Fred, aside from a couple of small on-screen appearances, mostly hid behind his puppets and piano. The formula was simple, thoughtful, and before long, wildly successful—so successful that NBC wanted to put a version of *The Children's Corner* on national television.

Despite the potential to reach more children on a bigger stage, Fred was wary. He was unwilling to walk away from the WQED program. Plus, he and Joanne now had two young sons, so he didn't love the idea of being away from home every week to film on set in New York. Most critically, Fred knew from his years at NBC that a commercial station had fundamentally different goals than those he was pursuing through public educational television.

But eventually, Fred agreed to give it a shot—with some strict stipulations. They could do a once-a-week program, and they'd have to film on Saturdays. He insisted on flying in and out on the same day to avoid missing seminary classes during the week or church with his family on Sundays.

When NBC agreed to his terms, filming began. Once again, the show took off. According to Josie's recollection, "They immediately broke the record for fan mail for a children's program on any station."[25]

But Fred's initial misgivings soon proved true. NBC was eager to capitalize on the success with show-inspired toys and children-focused ads during the program. Fred, vehemently opposed to any marketing aimed at children, dug in his heels.

When higher-ups at the station realized they would never change his mind, they pulled the show after just thirty-nine weeks. Fred was content. Josie was dismayed.

Back in Pittsburgh, tensions mounted between the pair as they continued to cohost the daily version of *Corner*. Josie, an entertainer at heart, had always enjoyed the unscripted and spontaneous nature of their show. But Fred was first and foremost an educator, and he was becoming increasingly adamant about planning every detail of the program.

"It got so that Fred started to worry about wording," said Josie. "You never fight with Fred. But once we had a twenty-minute discussion about whether to use the word would, should, or could."[26]

And then there was the baby-in-the-glove-compartment incident.

On a comedy show on Pittsburgh's commercial station, KDKA, Josie participated in a skit about a mother who had misplaced her baby. "Oh, where was the last place you saw it?" Josie asked in the sketch. "I think it's in the glove compartment of a car that was headed to Cleveland," quipped the other actor.[27]

Josie considered it nothing more than a harmless joke. Fred considered it cruel.

"Do you realize," he asked her, "that it's one of the worst things you can tell a child? A child is so afraid of being left or lost, and it's such an enclosed place, the glove compartment. That child is going to feel that he's being put into a small place—that he's lost his parents."

Josie tried to defend herself: "I said, 'Hey, it's a joke. It's a silly program. The kids know it's silly.' [But] Fred thought it was just horrible."[28]

Fred viewed Josie as a close friend, but he was beginning to think their philosophical differences were simply too great to overcome. In 1961, after eight years of working on the show, Fred walked away from *The Children's Corner*, claiming he wanted more time to focus on his studies at Pittsburgh Theological Seminary.

But years later, his wife Joanne would reveal the real reason for his decision. Fred felt he could "fashion a much better program for young children" and that "his work with Josie Carey, as popular and successful as it had been, wasn't the right road to his future."[29]

His instincts were right. Two years later, Fred Rogers would be a seminary graduate, an ordained minister, and a huge national celebrity—in Canada.

want you to be on camera."

Fred Rogers had just arrived in Toronto when Fred Rainsberry, the head of children's programming for the Canadian Broadcasting Corporation, made the unexpected demand.

"Oh…" stalled Fred. "I thought you wanted me to come and do puppets and music, which is what I've always done."

"No, you can do that too," said Rainsberry with a wave of his hand. "But I want you to look into the lens and just pretend that's a child, and we'll just call it *Misterogers*. Let's just do that."[30]

It wasn't what Fred had in mind when he accepted the invitation to create his own program in Canada, but he didn't argue. At least he would finally have a budget to create the show he wanted.

It seems the idea to play some sort of fictional on-air character for the show never occurred to Fred. "He just couldn't be anything but himself," recalled one coworker fondly. And it was immediately apparent that Fred, as himself, "managed [being on camera] very, very comfortably and easily…He was so focused on doing the right thing by his audience that he wasn't anxious."[31]

And when the cameras cut off, that genuine concern for his young viewers didn't. After dinner and bedtime with the boys, he and Joanne would often sit together at the kitchen table, reading and responding to fans' letters. He refused to outsource even this basic act of kindness.

Day after day, Fred wrote and filmed episodes of *Misterogers*. Night after night, he answered letters. And month after month, the show continued to grow. Before he knew it, four years had passed, and the Rogers family faced a big decision: Their Canadian visas were set to expire. Were they ready to make the move permanent?

Fred had finally created a wildly successful show on a network that understood his vision for serving children, but he was acutely attuned to the needs of the little people in his own home too. He knew his family was homesick for Pittsburgh. Asking them to become Canadian citizens for his sake felt unfair.

And so, after four wonderful years, Fred walked away from his dream job. There is no record of hesitation on his part. He may have thought the proven success of *Misterogers* in Canada would make it easier to find a place for a similar show in the US. But those hopes were quickly dashed.

Back in Pittsburgh, the leadership at his home station of WQED said they didn't have the funding for him to bring a version of *Misterogers* to the States. They promised to let him know if anything changed.

Fred held out hope for a phone call with good news, but the weeks stretched on, and he soon felt adrift. He started volunteering at Bellefield Presbyterian Church, using Daniel Tiger and his other puppets to teach preschool classes just so he could keep engaging with young children.

After a while, his parents began to worry. It's easy to imagine that secretly, Fred did too. Were his best career days now behind him, back in Toronto? If he couldn't find funding soon, how would he live out his ordained calling and work for "the broadcasting of grace throughout the land"?[32]

But then that train of thought sparked an idea—or, rather, a memory from his ordination ceremony. "We, as the Church…charge you to speak to us to remind us that we too, through you, must be involved," Bill Barker had said.[33]

What better time than now to do exactly that? Invigorated by the idea that the Church could be his partner in television ministry, Fred wrote an impassioned plea to the Presbytery board.

He began with some observations about the amount of time young children—"children whom the Church has never been able to reach!"—spend watching television. They're "being fed slick, stimulating, sound-tracked trash 1,000 hours a year while our Church schools try to teach the opposite with posters, crayons, and paste in one-tenth the time," he argued.

"We must know that we are failing our children," he went on. "But either we won't let ourselves admit it, or we think that there's nothing we as the Church can do about it."

Building to a crescendo, he laid out his request: "There IS something we can do!…Let's find the money to produce and promote long-range excellence in children's television. What a magnificent ministry it really can be!"[34]

The letter was incredibly moving—and yet the board remained unmoved. Ceremoniously ordaining Fred for ministry on television was one thing. Funding it was another thing entirely. With the Presbytery's rejection, Fred was back at square one.

Then, finally, his manager called with some good news: He'd scraped together enough support to fund the launch of a fifteen-minute show called *Mister Rogers' Neighborhood*, to air on WQED and other public television stations across the country. The money wouldn't last long, but it was enough to get started.

Fred, confident that the network would finance more episodes once the show was underway, got to work. But once again, he was wrong. Within one year, funding for the program ran out.

That would've been the end of *Mister Rogers' Neighborhood* and quite possibly Fred's career if not for one fiercely dedicated group: moms.

After just one year of watching *Neighborhood*, children across America had formed a special bond with Mister Rogers. "I remember sitting with a little boy who actually broke down in tears [at the news of the cancellation]," one staff member recalled.[35] That boy's mom and the mothers of thousands of other children wouldn't let *Neighborhood* be canceled without a fight.

First, letters of complaint poured in. Then, rallies and protests popped up at educational television stations from coast to coast. Moms in Boston went door-to-door raising money for the show. In Los Angeles, ten thousand superfans showed up at the local TV station for a chance to meet their favorite television neighbor, causing traffic jams as the line to meet Fred stretched across town.

Fred moved through the crowds like a modern-day Jesus in a cardigan—comfortable in the fray and unmoved by the frenzied concerns of staff members as he knelt down to connect with each child.

Finally, the massive swells of support caught the eyes of leaders at the Sears-Roebuck Foundation. They had been looking for a way to align the Sears brand with high-quality children's programming, and given the public outcry for more Mister Rogers, they were confident they had found their man.

After a few calls and some brief negotiations, an announcement was made.

Mister Rogers was coming back to the small screen, this time with a full thirty-minute program called *Mister Rogers' Neighborhood* that would be broadcast across the United States.

The news came not a moment too soon. Even as the mothers rejoiced, they had no idea just how important Fred would soon become in helping their children cope with world events. The nation was about to enter one of the most chaotic years in American history.

CHAPTER 7

Fred Rogers, glancing over at his friend in the church pew beside him, was shocked. The pastor in the pulpit, a man in his eighties, had just wrapped up what Fred called "the most poorly crafted sermon I had ever heard in my life."

And yet, there was his friend, wiping tears from her eyes. "He said exactly what I needed to hear," she whispered.

That terrible sermon? Exactly what she needed to hear? Fred thought in disbelief.

Later, he realized, "The Holy Spirit was able to translate the words of that feeble sermon to speak to the need of my friend...That experience changed my life. Ever since, I've been able to recognize that the space between someone who is offering the best he can and someone who is in need is Holy Ground."[36]

That included, in Fred's opinion, the space between the television set and each viewer. Humbled by that Sunday morning experience, Fred began to pray that the Holy Spirit might take his own feeble attempts and use them for the glory of God and the good of others.

Of course, Fred wasn't delivering sermons over public television. He couldn't even speak about his faith explicitly. But that didn't matter. "You can be an agent of what's good and not be terribly direct about it," reasoned Fred.[37]

And in 1968, the world needed whatever good it could find.

As young soldiers waged war in Vietnam, protesters in the United States took to the streets to wage war on war itself. At the same time, young lives were being lost in the country's other ongoing battle, the fight for the civil rights of Black Americans. The demand for justice and the backlash from white supremacists was reaching a fever pitch, especially in the weeks surrounding the assassination of Martin Luther King, Jr.

The country was riddled with hate, fear, and racial division—qualities that had no place in the kingdom of God or, as far as Fred was concerned, in *Mister Rogers' Neighborhood.*

In his very first week of episodes on the new, fully funded program, Fred invited a Black teacher and an interracial group of young students into his home, sending a clear message that all were welcome in his neighborhood.

Then, Fred took that message a step further, pushing back against segregation laws that prohibited Black Americans from swimming in public pools.

"He invited me to come over and to rest my feet in the water with him," explained actor François Clemmons. As Officer Clemmons, he was the first Black man with a recurring role in a children's television series. "The icon Fred Rogers not only was showing my brown skin in the tub with his white skin as two friends, but as I was getting out of that tub, he was helping me dry my feet."[38]

In the episode, the camera parks on a close-up shot of the men's feet side by side in the kiddie pool before Fred shares his towel with his friend. "Sometimes, just a minute like this will really make a difference," says Fred, gently splashing his feet.[39]

If viewers are reminded of another Teacher famously washing the feet of his friends, it's not an accident.

"What a tough job to try to communicate the gift of Jesus Christ to anybody. It can't be simply talked about, can it?" Fred asked in a letter to a friend. "Jesus himself used parables—so I guess that's our directive: try to show the kingdom of God through stories as much as possible."[40]

Though he often agonized over seemingly small choices, desperate to get his message precisely right, Fred also knew that only the Holy Spirit could take that message and translate it into what the viewer most needed to see or hear.

"When I walk in that studio door each day, I say, 'Dear God, let some word that is heard be Yours,'" explained Fred. "I always pray that through whatever we produce (whatever we say and do) some word that is heard might ultimately be God's word. That's my main concern."[41]

"So the show is like your church?" asked a journalist.

It wasn't a church, Fred replied, so much as "an atmosphere that allows people to be comfortable enough to be who they are...If people are comfortable in that atmosphere, they can grow from there in their own way. A lot of this—all of this—is just tending soil."[42]

And as Fred was tending the soil, God was clearly "[giving] the growth" (1 Corinthians 3:7, esv).

Take the story of a young boy whose "parents wouldn't even give him a winter blanket and wouldn't give him a bed to sleep in." As Fred shared with a reporter, the boy "found the *Neighborhood* and watched that program as he was growing up. He said that it gave him hope. He never knew that there were such kind people until he tuned into the *Neighborhood*."[43] But once he did, he found the courage to call an abuse hotline. His parents were sent to jail, and he was ultimately adopted.

Or think, perhaps, of the young mother who thanked Fred for saving her life. Overwhelmed by exhaustion and untreated postpartum depression, she was stopped at an intersection when she had an idea: It would be so easy to drift into the path of oncoming traffic and end her suffering.

But then, from the back seat, her sixteen-month-old began to sing, "It's a beautiful day in the neighborhood..." The song was a pinpoint of light in the darkness. Her foot returned safely to the brake, and when she got home, she finally reached out for the help she needed.

"How could a simple program like ours do all this?" Fred asked in awe after hearing these stories and many more like them. "But again, the Holy Spirit can use anything."[44]

After seven years of "tending soil" on *Neighborhood*, Fred was beginning to see the fruit of his labor, both spiritually and professionally. His was now the most popular show on PBS, and he had the creative freedom, life-changing impact, and vehicle for service of which he'd always dreamed.

No one ever suspected that he was about to throw it all away.

CHAPTER 8

It wouldn't be fair to call it a midlife crisis. Fred wasn't numbing existential dread with a new convertible or illicit affair. But his announcement sent out shockwaves all the same.

In 1975, after producing 455 episodes of *Mister Rogers' Neighborhood* in just seven years, Fred announced he was quitting the show to try something new. He wanted to produce television for adults.

Perhaps he thought he'd make a greater impact speaking to children's caregivers directly. Perhaps he was simply bored. "I'm not sure Fred really knew why he was doing [it]," admitted one coworker.[45]

But as he conducted interviews with politicians, artists, athletes, and psychologists for his new program, one thing became clear very quickly: This was not going to work. The gentleness, patience, and intentionality that made Fred a hero among children felt stilted and awkward to adult audiences more accustomed to fast-paced television.

He tried various formats and specials, but after four years with no real traction, Fred was ready to call it quits.

Then, a little boy jumped from a building.

"In the newspaper, I came across this little blurb that a child had jumped off a roof with a towel," recalled David Newell ("Mr. McFeely"), who read the story to Fred in the back of a taxi.[46] The child, convinced he could fly after watching Superman on TV, was hospitalized with his injuries.

Fred was appalled, filled with righteous anger at what he considered an egregious abuse of the very medium he felt called to redeem. By the time the cab ride was over, so was his retirement from children's television.

Mister Rogers' Neighborhood relaunched at the start of 1980. Still heartbroken by the little boy who believed he was Superman, Fred dedicated his first week back to showing the fictional nature of superhero movies. But he quickly moved on to topics most adults shied away from discussing with young children—topics like adoption, divorce, and death.

"Some things I don't understand," he'd tell his young viewers, but "whatever is mentionable can be more manageable."[47]

Fred had always believed life is for service, and now he knew beyond a shadow of a doubt that his children's program was his avenue for service. With renewed energy and commitment, Fred began to build a routine that would allow him to keep up with the demands of his calling for the next couple of decades.

Every day, Fred woke up between 4:30 and 5:30 in the morning to read his Bible and pray. He'd reference his schedule, praying for each person he expected to encounter that day, and then continue with thanking God for each name on his prayer list.

It was a long list, and his prayers often continued as he left home for the Pittsburgh Athletic Association, where he'd go for his morning swim. If anyone was standing near the water, they might have heard his quiet song of praise, "Jubilate Deo, jubilate Deo, alleluia" (Rejoice in the Lord, rejoice in the Lord, alleluia), right before he dove in.[48]

After swimming laps for forty-five minutes, Fred would shower and pause at the scale before heading to work. Remarkably, that scale read the exact same number every day of Fred's adult life: 143 pounds.

Then he'd head to WQED, greet the crew around 8:30, and go into makeup at 9:30. There, his ophthalmologist or her assistant would be waiting to put in his contact lenses. (At the end of the day, they'd also help remove them. Fred hated the process and was never comfortable touching his own eye.)

Taping would run from 10:00 to 4:30, with a break for lunchtime, at which point Fred would slip away to read his mail or meditate in the quiet of his office.

Some days, his son Jim recalled, if filming took a little longer, it "would be hectic in the evening because [Fred] was rushing home from work, in order to sit down with us for dinner" by 6:00. But when Fred made it home by 5:00, he "took a nap. We were told, 'You don't have to take a nap; it's not nap time, it's just quiet time. You can do whatever you want, but you do it quietly.'"[49]

After spending the evening with his family, Fred was in bed and asleep by 9:30 each night, always ensuring he had enough time for seven to eight uninterrupted hours of rest. Even his email address—zzz143@aol.com—was a nod to his love of sleep.

The next morning, he'd wake up and begin again. "There wasn't a spontaneous bone in that man's body," recalled one member of the *Neighborhood* staff.[50]

Despite his fairly regimented schedule, Fred was never hurried. Those who worked with him were often pleasantly surprised by how relaxed he was.

Michael Keaton, for example, was delighted when he discovered Fred's "sneaky, sly, great sense of humor."[51] Before he was a famous actor in his own right, Keaton worked as a stagehand at WQED where he once hid on set behind the "Picture-Picture" movie wall during filming.

When Fred moved to insert a video, the slot snapped open and a booming voice called out: "I will hear your confession now, son." Rogers joined the whole crew in laughing hysterically at the interruption, adding it to a list of Keaton's pranks that Rogers would recount with a smile for years to come.

Even though he was extremely disciplined in his work, Fred always had time to offer a smile or, even more often, a listening ear. His coworkers and friends noticed the way "everything decompressed and slowed down" when they were with him. They called it "Fred time."[52]

"Relationships are more important than anything else and [Fred] understood that if you're rushing around from one thing to another, you will invest nothing in the relationship," explained one of Fred's collaborators.[53]

Dan Fales, executive producer for WQED, once recalled experiencing that otherworldly "Fred time" on an elevator. Overwhelmed by production crises and phones ringing off the hook, he was impatiently stabbing at the elevator buttons when Fred got on.

Seeing the stress on Dan's face, Fred hit the elevator's stop button to offer some quiet encouragement: "Dan, remember what is important—your wonderful family, your sense of joy, and that wit that we all like. I hear that you work things out very well."[54]

That quiet moment made all the difference in Dan's day. Being with Fred usually did.

But you didn't have to be in an elevator with Fred to experience the love of God within him. As one little girl was about to discover, that love could be felt through a TV signal. And it might even work miracles right on your living room floor.

CHAPTER 9

As Kathy Usher watched her daughter Beth walk into class on the first day of school, she—like all moms—was hoping her child would thrive in kindergarten. A few weeks later, she was just hoping Beth would survive.

The nightmare began on the playground where, after falling off the seesaw, Beth had her first seizure. A few days later, she had her second. And then her third. By the time they got a diagnosis—a "one-in-ten-million brain disease"—Beth was suffering through a hundred seizures a day.[55]

"The only way my mom could shower and dress for work without worrying was to prop me up with soft pillows and place me in front of the television," recalled Beth. "She usually turned on *Mister Rogers' Neighborhood*, and for the length of the show I never had a single seizure."[56]

Every single weekday for two years, Fred's program brought a miraculous thirty-minute reprieve from Beth's unremitting suffering.

So when doctors said a bright young surgeon, Dr. Ben Carson, would need to perform a high-risk surgery to remove half of Beth's brain, Kathy called WQED to request a signed photo of Mister Rogers for her daughter.

When the secretary approached Fred with a photo to sign, he insisted she call Kathy back right away. "Will you be home this evening at 7:00? Fred would like to call and speak with Beth," the secretary told Kathy.[57]

And right on time, he did.

"I took the phone from my mother and said hello," Beth recalled. "I heard a familiar voice and felt immediately at ease." For nearly an hour, Beth sat in her family's kitchen and talked to Fred about everything from her fear of dying to her longing for friends.

Around the corner, her parents hovered quietly in the hallway, listening in as tears streamed down their faces.

"I love you, Mister Rogers," Beth said as the call came to a close.[58]

Shortly after Beth's twelve-hour surgery, Fred called again. "How is she doing?" he wanted to know. The surgery itself had gone fine, explained Kathy, but Beth had since slipped into a coma. A worried Fred called every day for two weeks before finally asking if he could fly out to visit them in Baltimore. When Kathy agreed, he immediately bought a ticket and arrived the very next day.

With Beth still in a coma, Fred put on a private puppet show and prayed for her; then he slipped away, leaving behind his puppets as a special gift for Beth to awaken to—which she did, a few weeks later.

"Praise God," breathed Fred with relief when Kathy called with the news.

Throughout the ordeal and the lifelong friendship with Beth that followed, very few people even knew it had happened. Fred was diligent in his efforts to keep the story from the press.

In fact, almost all the stories of Fred's incredible compassion—and there are so very many—took place off-screen.

There was the time when Fred looked out the window and saw a man who had just been mugged limping away on the New York City street below. Fred rushed downstairs to hand the man a hundred-dollar bill. "I just want you to know that somebody in this world loves you," said Fred.[59]

Or the time he showed up at his coworker's front door unexpectedly. "I was praying, and I felt you needed some help," he told Lisa Hamilton. He had no idea she had become a widow that very morning.

"I was really panicky," she said of the morning she awoke, still holding her husband's hand, to discover he had lost his battle with cancer during the night. But then, Fred appeared out of nowhere. "Fred Rogers is the person who called the funeral home, and he wept with me over [my husband's] body— the only person I remember weeping with me."[60]

Fred was never one to shy away from people's pain or avoid what others might consider an uncomfortable interaction. Sometimes, the results were downright miraculous.

Fred's secretary once watched as he knelt down to connect with a twelve-year-old boy with autism whose family had never heard him speak. Fred "had the King and Queen puppets on his hands, and…the child started speaking in full sentences to the King and Queen," she explained. "The father started blubbering to the point where he could no longer hold the camera."[61]

Most of Fred's young friends never appeared on *Neighborhood*, but there were some memorable exceptions.

Jeff Erlanger was five years old when he first met Mister Rogers. Confined to a wheelchair, he was getting ready to undergo a major surgery to fuse his spine when his parents wrote to Fred, asking if he'd be willing to meet their son. He did—off camera and under the radar as he had with so many other children.

But a few years later, when Fred wanted to have a child in a wheelchair on an episode of *Neighborhood*, he remembered Jeff's incredible maturity and asked his staff to call the Erlangers.

In the episode, it's easy to see why Fred wanted his viewers to meet this particular young boy. With a matter-of-fact tone and a smile, Jeff talks about the tumor that made him a quadriplegic and the wheelchair he's had since he was four.

Then, the two launch into an impromptu duet of Fred's song "It's You I Like."

"It's you I like, the way you are right now, the way down deep inside you, not the things that hide you—not your fancy chair," they improvise with a shared laugh. "That's just beside you, but it's you I like, every part of you."[62]

Twenty years later, in 1999, the pair crossed paths once more. Fred was decked out in a tux, about to be inducted into the Television Hall of Fame, when Jeff rolled onto the stage. Fred, unable to contain his joy, leaped from his seat to join him.

"I'm so happy to see you! Thank you for coming—what a surprise!" said Fred, leaning over to embrace his friend.[63]

When the rapturous applause finally ceased, Jeff looked at Fred and said, "You know, when you tell people that 'it's you I like,' we know that you really mean it. And today, I want to let you know, on behalf of millions of children and grown-ups, that it's you I like."[64]

The tears on the faces of everyone in the room said more about Fred than the award itself ever could.

Two years later, Fred would retire from television. Millions of children would sit down to watch the last episode of *Mister Rogers' Neighborhood* on August 30, 2001. At almost the exact same time, terrorists were purchasing tickets for four transcontinental flights they planned to hijack. Fred's work wasn't done quite yet.

CHAPTER 10

On October 23, 2001, Fred Rogers sat down at the piano and turned to face the camera as he had so many times before. But when the recording light began blinking red, his usual warm smile was nowhere to be seen.

It had been over a month since hijackers crashed planes in both New York and Pennsylvania, the two states Fred called home for most of his life. But he still looked dazed and confused.

"Fred, what's wrong?" asked producer Margy Whitmer. "I just don't know what good these are going to do," Fred admitted, tears filling his eyes.

"When the horror of 9/11 really hit him, I think it was a real eye-opener," explained Whitmer later. "He was realizing it was just so big. It's always going to be an ongoing struggle to overcome evil."[65]

As God would have it, Fred's thirty-three-year career on *Neighborhood* was bookended by two of the most difficult years in American history. His first episode premiered amid the chaos of 1968, a year in which he pushed back against racism and helped young children voice their questions about the assassination of public figures.

Now, more than nine hundred episodes later, he was coming out of his short-lived retirement to help those once-small viewers—all grown up now with children of their own—shepherd the next generation in the aftermath of the deadliest terrorist attack on US soil.

"No matter what our particular job, especially in our world today, we all are called to be 'tikkun olam,' repairers of creation," he told viewers. "Thank you for whatever you do, wherever you are, to bring joy and light and hope and faith and pardon and love to your neighbor and to yourself."[66]

It was reminiscent of a message he often gave in times of tragedy: "When I was a little boy and something bad happened in the news, my mother would tell me to look for the helpers. 'You'll always find people helping,' she'd say. And I've found that that's true. In fact, it's one of the best things about our wonderful world."[67]

After recording the series of post-9/11 messages, Fred paused to play a soft tune on the piano, the chords a mix of melancholy and hope, before stepping away from the studio for good.

That's not to say Fred was done working. Even in "retirement," he held on to the belief that life is for service. When he wasn't traveling around the country for speaking engagements, he was working with fifteen employees to develop a children's media center at Saint Vincent College in his hometown of Latrobe, where he hoped to spend his final years developing educational programs for modern families.

But it was not meant to be. This work—and his legacy—would have to be carried on by those who came after him.

In October 2002, just weeks after his final 9/11 video aired on the first anniversary of the tragedy, Fred Rogers was diagnosed with stomach cancer.

Unwilling to cancel commitments he'd made to appear in public over the holidays, Fred put off surgery until January 2003. By then, it was too late. Doctors removed his entire stomach, but the cancer had already spread.

"He was just so exhausted," Joanne recalled of the days and weeks following the surgery. "And he said, 'I hope they don't think I'm being elitist to not have [friends] visiting'; and he cried when he said that because he didn't want to hurt their feelings."

He tried to write emails to the many people he loved but often fell asleep before he could finish the task. Despite his frustrations and exhaustion, he did manage to reach out to a few close friends.

"He told me that he was sick," recalled Yo-Yo Ma, the famous cellist and personal friend to Fred. "I played a Bach Sarabande for him over the phone."[68]

Fred used the little energy he had left to arrange for handpicked personal belongings to be mailed to particular friends and family after his death. The gifts would have to say what he could not.

Joanne, heartbroken by her husband's pain and her own impending loss, did her best to ease his worries. "Fred," she said, sitting on the bed beside him, "I know the boys are going to be okay. I'll try to be."

"Oh, Joanne, you don't know what a relief that is for me to hear that," he replied.[69]

Just a few weeks after his surgery, on February 27, 2003, he was gone.

At the funeral, Reverend Bill Barker—the friend who had stood up for Fred in front of the Presbytery board so many years before—stood up for him once more, this time to give the eulogy in front of the more than 2,700 attendees.

Fred was laid to rest in his beloved "clergy tie," a fitting reminder of his life's work and calling. As a member of the "royal priesthood," Fred had worked wholeheartedly to restore creation, one small act of kindness at a time, in his own little neighborhood (1 Peter 2:9).

In the end, it wasn't the awards he won or the number of viewers he reached that made his life extraordinary. It was the everyday ways in which he loved.

"He was one of the most authentic and Christlike people that I have ever known in my life," said one colleague. "Everyone you talk to that had any encounter with him: It was a real moment in their lives."[70]

"What most people couldn't see in Fred was his enormous power. Power. Capital P," said another. "Fred is the most powerful person I have ever known in my whole life…His power derived from a really unique place. It was his absolute self-possession, which is very different from self-interest or self-satisfaction, or selfishness. He didn't need anything from you or from me."[71]

Free of the need to take, Fred was able to give—a listening ear, a warm smile—but most of all, an invitation to be loved.

As Fred himself put it, "'Won't You Be My Neighbor?' [is] an invitation for somebody to be close to you. I think everybody longs to be loved and longs to know that he or she is lovable. And consequently, the greatest thing that we can do is to help somebody know that they're loved and capable of loving."[72]

That is the work of the everyday priest—and as Fred's life shows, it's the very work that can change someone's life forever.

THREE WAYS TO GLORIFY GOD IN YOUR WORK
AS SEEN IN THE LIFE OF FRED ROGERS

(Jordan) don't think I've ever heard of a more Jesus-like person than Fred Rogers. He was as one biographer put it, "Mother Teresa in a cardigan."[73] But if Rogers were here today, I'm confident he would remind us of two things. First, Jesus—not Fred—is the hero of this story. Second, the same Holy Spirit that empowered Rogers's extraordinary life now lives in you and me. So, we modern mere Christians can glorify God through our work in much the same way as Rogers did. How?

I. MERE CHRISTIANS GLORIFY GOD BY EMBRACING THEIR POSITION IN GOD'S "ROYAL PRIESTHOOD."

Before Christ, priests and Pharisees had a lock on which vocations did "the work of the Lord." But when Jesus, the Great High Priest, came to earth, he spent the vast majority of his life working not as a religious professional but as a mere carpenter.

That truth helps us understand what the apostle Peter said in 1 Peter 2:9 when he claimed that every follower of Christ is now a member of God's "royal priesthood." It's no longer just literal priests who represent God in the world and serve as conduits for his goodness. It's every carpenter, entrepreneur, and barista—*any* Christian doing genuinely good work.

How can that be true? Because God is now in each and every Christian through the power of his Holy Spirit. So, to quote the great preacher Charles Spurgeon, for the believer, "nothing is secular—everything is sacred," including your work as a mere Christian.[74]

Nobody embraced their position in God's royal priesthood more enthusiastically than Fred Rogers, who believed he could do God's work from behind a pulpit *or* a puppet—a conviction he literally took to his grave in the form of his "clergy tie."

But Fred wasn't just encouraged by the sacred label of his seemingly "secular" work. He glorified God by allowing that truth to shape his vocation. He worked hard at the "good works, which God prepared in advance" for him to do (Ephesians 2:10), even though, given his family's considerable wealth, he never had to work a day in his life. He used his platform to tell artistic parables of the kingdom of God. And he worked to be a priestly "repairer of creation," redeeming what he saw was broken in the medium of television.

Fred said that "deep within each of us is a spark of the divine just waiting to be used to light up a dark place."[75] That is true of you, believer. Like Fred Rogers, you can glorify God in the "dark place" you work by embracing your position in the "royal priesthood" and viewing your job as a primary place God has called you to "let your light shine before others" (Matthew 5:16).

Take a moment right now to thank God for drafting you into the "royal priesthood," and ask him to show you how specifically he is calling you to more faithfully represent him in your workplace.

2. MERE CHRISTIANS GLORIFY GOD BY MAKING TIME TO EXPERIENCE THEIR BELOVEDNESS.

Fred Rogers lived a *wildly* productive life. Over the course of *Mister Rogers' Neighborhood*'s thirty-one seasons, Fred personally wrote nine hundred scripts, two hundred songs, and thirteen operas. Even more impressive was how much time he spent personally showing compassion to thousands of hurting people off camera.

But here's what's most remarkable about Fred's productivity: He accomplished more than most people ever dream *while also* spending more time with his heavenly Father than most people ever dare.

He began each morning in silent prayer. At lunch, he would slip away to the quiet of his office to meditate. Upon arriving home from the studio, he would often spend another hour napping or praying before dinner.

As one of his friends put it, Fred "fiercely guarded his time of quiet and reflection."[76] And in this, he reflected his Savior who "often withdrew to lonely places and prayed" (Luke 5:16).

Like Jesus, Fred wasn't interested in silence for the sake of silence. "It wasn't just the absence of noise he advocated," said a close friend of Fred's, "but silence that reflects on the goodness of God."[77]

In other words, the spiritual discipline of solitude was a means to an end for Fred Rogers: regularly experiencing the extraordinary love God had for him. A sign in Fred's office explicitly reminded him of that love. It was a Hebrew printing of Song of Songs 2:16: "My beloved is mine and I am his."

It is precisely because Fred spent so much time quietly reflecting on his status as a "beloved" child of God that he was able to share love so freely with God's other children. "He didn't need anything from you or from me," reflected one of his coworkers.[78] Because his sense of belovedness led him to "the freedom of self-forgetfulness."[79]

The same can be true for you and me, believer. Like Fred, we will glorify God by making the time to abide in him and experience the belovedness that frees us to fully love our neighbors as ourselves (see John 15:1-8).

That could look like recommitting yourself to a morning "quiet time" before work, setting reminders to meditate on God's love throughout your day, or hanging a visual reminder of God's love in your office. Whatever works for you, works. But abide we must if we long to glorify God more fully in our work.

3. MERE CHRISTIANS GLORIFY GOD BY WORKING AT A PACE THAT ALLOWS THEM TO EXTEND GOD'S LOVE TO OTHERS.

It wasn't just a sense of belovedness that led Fred to demonstrate otherworldly kindness to others. It was also his extraordinary lack of hurry.

When Fred's biographer, Max King, was asked to sum up the message of Fred's life in a single phrase, he said, "Slow down, be kind." To Fred, those things were "directly related."[80] Because he understood that you and I must "slow down" *in order to* "be kind" and show God's love to those we work with. Which is why Fred urged anyone who would listen to put their "dominant energies into developing a sane design for living."[81]

Here again, Jesus served as the perfect model for Fred. As pastor John Mark Comer has pointed out, "If there's anything you pick up from reading the four Gospels, it's that Jesus was rarely in a hurry."[82] Even when a child's life hung in the balance, Jesus moved at a pace that allowed him to attend to the suffering of one daughter on his way to heal another (see Mark 5:21-43).

You and I will glorify God when we model Jesus's lack of hurry so that we can extend God's love to those we work with. And Fred Rogers shows us how to do that in a more modern context.

First, *budget tons of margin into your calendar*. If you think it's going to take thirty minutes to get to a meeting, budget forty-five. It is exactly this kind of margin that allowed Fred to see and engage with the pain in his coworkers' lives, like the time he pressed the stop button in the elevator to bless a fellow producer.

Second, *resolve to be with who you're with*. Not only did Fred not hurry, but also, when someone entered his presence, he offered *them* the gift of feeling unhurried. There was no checking his watch. No glancing at mail on his desk. When Fred was with someone, regular time stood still, "Fred time" began, and "urgency seemed to dissipate," as Fred made the other person feel like the image-bearer of God they were.[83] You can do the same today by silencing distractions and resolving to be fully present with who you're with.

Finally, *when you fail to be unhurried, choose the important over the urgent*. Fred became more human to me when I heard his son say that there were days when Fred "was rushing home from work, in order to sit down with [his family] for dinner."[84] As his biographer explains, even when Fred failed to have enough margin in his calendar, he "never—ever—let the urgency of work or life impede his focus on what he saw as basic human values: integrity, respect, responsibility…and of course…kindness."[85] God will be glorified when the same is said of you and me.

Want to share Fred Rogers's story with a friend?
Send them a free copy of this section of the book at
JordanRaynor.com/free.

FANNIE LOU HAMER

HOW TO GLORIFY GOD BY DOING JUSTICE LOVINGLY, TRUSTING
WHILE HUSTLING, AND HOPING THROUGH FAILURE

*Please note that this story contains a scene of sexual violence
that some readers may find distressing. If you or someone you know is
experiencing sexual violence, help is available. In the United States, you can
contact the National Sexual Assault Hotline at 1-800-656-HOPE (4673)
or visit RAINN.org for confidential support and resources.*

CHAPTER 11

When President Lyndon B. Johnson entered the Oval Office on August 22, 1964, he was a man on a mission. Election Day was just two months away, and the biggest threat to his victory was not the Republican nominee but a poor, Black, female sharecropper from Mississippi.

Johnson was determined to silence her.

At that very moment, Fannie Lou Hamer was less than two hundred miles away in Atlantic City, New Jersey, sliding into a modest belted dress she'd borrowed from a friend. In a few hours, she would testify in front of the Democratic National Convention (DNC).

She wasn't worried about President Johnson, and she certainly wasn't aware that he was worried about her. She was focused on her mission of convincing the DNC's Credentials Committee to unseat delegates from Mississippi's Democratic Party and replace them with delegates from the new Mississippi Freedom Democratic Party (MFDP), which Hamer helped form. Because in a state where the majority of the population was Black, Mississippi's elected delegates were nearly all members of the Ku Klux Klan.

It wasn't because Black Americans didn't have the right to vote. In other southern states, 50 to 70 percent of the Black population was registered. But in Hamer's home state, their voices were not being heard.

As she was about to testify, it wasn't for lack of trying. Simply registering to vote could get you beaten, raped, or murdered by members of the Democratic Party or even the police.

President Johnson knew what Hamer was preparing to say. He'd ordered the FBI to tap the phones of MFDP leaders, so he wasn't caught by surprise.

Publicly, he was a proponent of civil rights. He'd just signed the landmark Civil Rights Act of 1964 that very summer. But privately, he was far more concerned with winning, and he couldn't do that without the support of white Democrats in the South.

On the morning of August 22, that's who he picked up the phone to call. Working down his call sheet, Johnson tried desperately to reassure southern governors and other elected officials that the MFDP's challenge was of no concern. He had a plan, he told them, to neutralize Hamer and her friends.

But at 2:00 that afternoon, the doors to the Credentials Committee's meeting room swung open and hundreds of people poured in to hear the MFDP make their case. The crowd quickly filled every seat before lining up against the walls, and then up and down the aisles.

Above the fray, the press looked down from the viewing room. Cameramen from NBC got into position and checked their equipment. Even as they prepared to broadcast Hamer's testimony live, President Johnson was hatching an eleventh-hour plan to stop her.

At 3:00, the meeting began, and before long, Hamer was called upon to testify. Emerging from the crowded aisles, she approached the microphone, stepping into the view of the cameras.

Wasting no time, Hamer launched into her story even as she placed her white handbag on the table and lowered herself into the seat. "Mr. Chairman, my name is Mrs. Fannie Lou Hamer, and I live at 626 East Lafayette Street, Ruleville, Mississippi," she began.[1]

Even that simple statement was a bold act of defiance. She was about to detail the violent, bloody lengths to which white supremacists had gone to silence her, and yet she was giving out her home address on national TV. This was not a woman easily intimidated.

With sweat and determination on her brow, she continued in a clear, strong voice: "It was the 31st of August in 1962 that 18 of us traveled 26 miles to the county courthouse in Indianola to try to register to try to become first-class citizens."[2]

But before she could share the most horrific parts of her story, the broadcast abruptly ended.

President Johnson had called an impromptu press conference at the White House. Journalists, hoping for his long-awaited announcement of a running mate, cut away from Hamer to capture it. Instead of satisfying their curiosity, Johnson rambled on for a few minutes about the day John F. Kennedy was assassinated. The man clearly had nothing to say, but he'd managed to keep Hamer off air—that is, until his plan backfired.

The president failed to consider that NBC's cameras would continue to roll in Atlantic City, capturing Hamer's full testimony. Or that interrupting a live broadcast to say nothing would make people more interested in her testimony, not less.

As a result of Johnson's actions, Hamer's account would play in full on that night's evening news to a much larger audience. And over the next few days, highlights would air again and again.

All of America would hear her dramatic, gut-wrenching story and be forced to consider the question she posed at the conclusion of her testimony: "Is this America, the land of the free and the home of the brave? Where we have to sleep with our telephones off of the hooks because our lives be threatened daily because we want to live as decent human beings, in America?"[3]

In the years since, Hamer's testimony from that day—and her tireless work that followed—has been hailed as a catalyst for securing the voting rights of Black Americans in Mississippi and beyond.

But her legacy is about much more than racial injustice, civil rights, and politics. It's a story that shows how mere Christians can glorify God by doing justice while refusing to hate the unjust, trusting God's sovereignty while also working hard, and lamenting failure in this world while waiting with hope for the kingdom to come. It is a story that continues to inspire Christians today to work with grace and grit—a gripping narrative you will not soon forget.

CHAPTER 12

Ella Townsend's scarred and calloused hands were on prickly cotton bolls as she worked her way down snow-white rows, but her mind was on the child in her womb.

Despite October's recent arrival, the sun was still bright in the sky, its heat amplified by the unrelenting humidity. And Ella, feeling the first twinges of labor as she dragged a hundred pounds of cotton alongside her, was praying for a miracle.

At forty-three years old, she understood that every birth is a miracle. But in 1917, none was more miraculous than that of a healthy Black child to a healthy Black mother in rural Mississippi, where one in four Black children were dying before their fifth birthday.

In Ella's personal experience, the odds were even worse. After nineteen pregnancies—and nineteen unmedicated, at-home births without a doctor present—she'd buried seven children, including the four babies she'd birthed in the last three years.

She had no reason to believe this one would be any different, but as her contractions grew and she headed for their small rental home, Ella held tightly to hope.

She didn't have to labor long before she heard it—the answer to her prayers, a loud cry from strong lungs. Fannie Lou Townsend had arrived. *Thank you, Lord*, breathed Ella with a cry of relief.

Over the next few years, Fannie Lou continued to beat the odds. First, she celebrated that landmark fifth birthday. Shortly thereafter, she survived a case of polio. Then she learned to read and write—a rare accomplishment for Black children who were allowed to attend school for only a few months each year.

Fannie Lou was her parents' pride and joy.

Her father Jim, a part-time minister, often invited her up front during church services to recite poetry and Bible verses. At mealtimes, he'd gather everyone around and then place young Fannie Lou up on the table so everyone could see and hear her sing:

> This little light of mine, I'm going to let it shine!
> This little light of mine, I'm going to let it shine!
> This little light of mine, I'm going to let it shine!
> Oh, let it shine, let it shine, let it shine!

At seven years old, Fannie Lou was baptized in the nearby Quiver River by visiting missionaries while both parents watched proudly from the riverbanks.

But all the pride, joy, and love in the world couldn't shield their youngest child from the harsh realities of their daily existence as sharecroppers.

With slavery technically outlawed in the United States, plantation owners would rent homes, land, and equipment to impoverished workers while promising a share of the profits from the crops they picked.

But at the end of the harvest season, many sharecroppers would discover that the exorbitant prices placed on their borrowed homes and tools exceeded their projected income. Now indebted to the very landowners who had enslaved their parents and grandparents, they were left wondering how to feed their own families.

"White people have clothes, they have food to eat, and we work all the time, and we don't have anything!" lamented young Fannie Lou to her mother.[4] "We worked all the time, just worked and then we would be hungry," she later recalled.[5] "We would just, you know, exist. Not really live, exist."[6]

But even worse than the unrelenting hunger was the fear that gnawed at her belly day and night.

Fannie Lou was only six years old when news of Joe Pullen swept through her community like wildfire. Pullen, a forty-year-old sharecropper who lived nearby, hadn't received the wages promised to him by plantation owner W.T. Saunders. So when Saunders gave Pullen some money to hire a few day laborers, the sharecropper kept the cash for himself.

Saunders was livid. With a friend in tow, he marched up to Pullen's front door and shot him in the arm. Pullen returned fire—with much more precise aim, despite his injury. Saunders fell dead at his feet.

It didn't take long for Saunders's friend to race to town and round up an angry mob while Pullen ran for safety three miles deep in the bayou. But the mob closed in, and a shoot-out ensued. The lone Pullen held his ground for hours until someone doused the swamp in gasoline and set it aflame.

Pullen was unconscious but still breathing when the mob pulled him from his hiding spot in a hollowed-out tree. With an unquenched thirst for blood, the men tied Pullen to a car, dragged him through the street, and then cut off his ear and displayed it like a trophy in a downtown shop window.

The murder traumatized Fannie Lou, and it wouldn't be the last time she heard adults whispering stories of horror above her head. After all, Mississippi recorded more lynchings than any other state in the country.

Like many children, Fannie Lou watched her parents for cues on how to survive in a world she didn't understand. "I used to hear [Mama] get on her knees and pray that God would let all her children live, praying she'd see all of them grown," she'd later explain. But Ella didn't just "let go and let God." When the morning sun came up, Ella "would carry her gun to the field" in a bucket for protection. "She was a deeply religious person, but she didn't allow anyone to mess with her children."[7]

On more than one occasion, she put her own safety on the line to protect her family. One time, a man rode out to the fields, intent on taking Ella's teenage niece back with him "to give her a good whipping."

"You don't have no Black children and you not goin' to beat no Black children," said Ella while Fannie Lou looked on with wide eyes. "If you step down off of that horse, I'll go to Hell and back with you before Hell can scorch a feather."[8]

In her mother's example, Fannie Lou was learning how to submit to God's will without submitting to injustice and how to walk in that tension without letting hate take root in her own heart.

But Ella couldn't protect her children forever. In 1930, an accident in the fields resulted in an eye infection. Unable to afford treatment, Ella lost her sight and her ability to work.

At thirteen years old, Fannie Lou was forced to quit school and work full time in her mother's place. Her childhood was over. Her adulthood—and first acts of protest—were about to begin.

CHAPTER 13

Fannie Lou Hamer was on her hands and knees, scrubbing a toilet that wasn't hers. Just because the fields weren't yet white with cotton didn't mean plantation owner W.D. Marlow would give her the day off.

"I had cleaned one bathroom and was working on another," recalled Hamer, when Marlow's daughter Maud appeared in the doorway. "You don't have to clean this one too good, Fannie Lou. It's just Ole Honey's."[9]

Hamer rocked back from her knees, letting those words sink in as Maud skipped away. The toilet in Hamer's rental home had never worked. Because Marlow refused to fix it, she was forced to use an outhouse with a rickety wooden door that trapped the stench and flies inside.

But just a few dozen steps away, Marlow's dog had an entire bathroom to himself.

Hamer was "mad enough to boil."[10]

For the next few weeks, she watched and waited. At last, the Marlows left home for an evening in town. Marching right past Ole Honey's toilet, Hamer made her way to the master bath and let the hot water flow.

It was her first bubble bath. "I used to have a real ball knowing they didn't want me in their tub...just relaxing in that bubble bath [whenever they would leave home]," Hamer would later confess.[11] "I would walk out feeling very proud, I just carried my little own protest, you know."[12]

Over time, Hamer grew bolder. When the Marlows told her she had to wait until they were done eating to partake in the very meals she'd prepared, she simply ate before calling them to the table.

"I would just eat and have myself a time," she later said. "I would eat out all of the spoons and watch them eat behind me."[13]

"I was rebelling in the only way I knew how to rebel," Hamer said of her unseen acts of resistance. "I just steady hoped for a chance that I could really lash out, and say what I had to say about what was going on in Mississippi."[14]

And in Mississippi, white supremacists were guarding a whole lot more than their own bathrooms and kitchens. They were also guarding the voting booth.

It had been seventy-five years since Congress had passed the Fifteenth Amendment stating that "the right of citizens of the United States to vote shall not be denied or abridged by the United States or by any State on account of race, color, or previous condition of servitude."[15]

But Mississippi had wasted no time amending its own state constitution in response. By enacting burdensome poll taxes and complicated literacy tests on Black Americans wishing to register, white supremacists ensured very few even tried. And those who did risked serious harm.

During the 1946 election, one Mississippi senator called on his fellow Ku Klux Klansmen to "use any means" to keep Black voters away from the polls. "You do it the night before the election," he declared in a public speech. "If you don't understand what that means, you are just plain dumb."[16]

Anyone who refused to be intimidated by violent threats the night before Election Day would find Klansmen with guns waiting to assault them at the polls. Their strong-arm tactics were so successful that many, including Hamer, didn't even realize they had a legal right to vote.

As a result, white supremacists retained all power in a state where they were outnumbered by Black citizens. With that power, Mississippi lawmakers codified racist statutes that set up even more obstacles to voter registration, laid the groundwork to abolish public schools rather than integrate them, and even outlawed civil rights activism altogether.

With each new law, standing up for justice became more and more dangerous. "There's open season on the Negroes now," one Mississippi resident told a reporter. "[Anyone] who wants to go out and shoot himself one…we'll free him."[17]

This wasn't baseless boasting. Just twenty-five miles east of Hamer's home, two white supremacists tortured and murdered fourteen-year-old Emmett Till for flirting with a white woman named Carol Bryant (though, decades later, Bryant would confess to lying about the encounter).

The men, who would later brag publicly about the murder, were acquitted by an all-white jury after a kangaroo court trial and an hour of deliberation.

"We wouldn't have taken so long if we hadn't stopped to drink pop," remarked one juror with a laugh.[18]

No one ever did time for the murder, despite it being one of the most widely reported lynching cases in the state. Many more never made national headlines.

On the Marlow plantation, sharecroppers swapped stories of National Association for the Advancement of Colored People (NAACP) leaders being run out of town, assaulted, and worse. Hamer was careful to keep her own small acts of protest—and the anger burning within her—a secret from her bosses.

"We would smile and that would just fool 'em," she later said. "We been some of the greatest actors on earth."[19]

But there are limits to what a smile can hide or a bubble bath can fix. And white supremacists were about to push Fannie Lou Hamer too far.

CHAPTER 14

How can it be that my mother had twenty children, her mother had twenty, and I can't even have one? Fannie Lou Hamer had just given birth, but the only cry in the room was her own.

Twice now, she had watched her body grow along with her hope, only for her labor pains to usher in death rather than life. And then there were the miscarriages—losses that came so early she never even felt the joy of kicks in her womb.

It all felt so unfair.

Ever since marrying Pap Hamer in 1944, Fannie Lou wanted nothing more than to be a mother. The opportunity had come sooner than she imagined when an infant daughter in the community needed a home. Her initial joy at becoming a mother by adoption was soon mixed with more complex emotions as their efforts to grow their small family further only resulted in loss after loss.

Then, five years into their marriage and struggles with infertility, Pap approached Fannie Lou with some devastating news. He was going to be a father. He'd had an affair with a woman across town, and she was going to have the one thing Hamer wanted most: his child.

There are no records of how Hamer responded at that moment or how she came to terms with his betrayal, but somehow she did. The couple stayed together, and she kept praying for a miracle.

But after her second stillbirth, lying in bed in a small, hot room that was all too quiet, Hamer was struggling to hold on to hope. Her mother Ella, blind to the world but not her youngest daughter's pain, sat by her side in the darkness. But even that small comfort would soon be gone.

Over the following years, Ella's health deteriorated further and further until finally, in 1961, she slipped away in her sleep.

Hamer moved through her days in a fog. The only things that could cut through the haze of her grief were the sharp abdominal stabs that struck without warning, often leaving her doubled over and breathless.

Pap, feeling helpless at his wife's emotional and physical suffering, pleaded with her to go to a doctor. Too sick and tired to argue, she relented. And it was there, in the doctor's office, that Hamer finally got answers to questions she'd been asking for over a decade.

Noncancerous tumors on her uterus were the source of her painful periods, abdominal pain, and perhaps her long struggle with infertility. With surgery, the doctor assured her, all these problems could go away.

There was, at last, some hope.

But in the weeks following the surgery, Hamer began experiencing symptoms far beyond what was normal for recovery—menopausal symptoms like hot flashes, mood swings, and insomnia. She may never have known why if not for her friend, a cook on the Marlow plantation.

The friend had overheard Marlow's wife having a conversation about Hamer's procedure. The doctor hadn't just removed tumors. He'd removed her entire uterus in a complete hysterectomy done without her knowledge or consent.

Hamer's dreams of having her own children were now utterly and truly dead.

"I was very angry about what had been done to me," she later said. "[The doctor] should have told me. I would have loved to have children." When she confronted her doctor about the rumor, his bored expression said it all. "I asked him. Why? Why had he done that to me? He didn't have to say nothing—and he didn't."[20]

In the years to come, Hamer would learn that this barbarous act—what Hamer called a "Mississippi appendectomy"—was a widespread practice white supremacists used to sterilize women of color. "Six out of the ten Negro women that go to the hospital [in Sunflower County] are sterilized with their tubes tied," she later estimated.[21] The practice would continue throughout the American South into the early 1970s.

As her body slowly recovered from the major operation, her spirit did not. Throughout the winter of 1962, Hamer stopped pasting on a smile as white-hot rage brewed beneath her stoic exterior.

She didn't want to be silent anymore. Sneaking bubble baths and bites of food was no longer enough. But what else could she do?

Then, amid her grief and anger, she heard of a new organization setting up shop in her hometown of Ruleville. The group was called the Student Nonviolent Coordinating Committee, but everyone called it SNCC (pronounced "snick") for short.

Ruleville had never had an organized civil rights group before, but it wasn't as if Hamer could just walk into town and sign up. As one civil rights leader put it, "Mississippi isn't the rest of the South...You sit in over in Nashville, you go to jail. Sit in here, they'll bash your brains in, murder your family, and then put you in jail."[22]

The group's work was barely underway when Herbert Lee, a Black man who had volunteered to help, was shot and killed in broad daylight in front of a dozen witnesses. The only Black witness who was willing to testify about what had happened was quickly murdered too. The shooter, of course, was acquitted.

Hamer was angry, but that didn't mean she had a death wish. So she waited. As a Christian, she'd been taught to wait on God, to pray like the prophet Amos: *Let judgment run down as waters, and righteousness as a mighty stream, Lord!* (see Amos 5:24).

If she was going to do more than that, to put her very life on the line for what she believed to be right, it was going to take a sign from God.

CHAPTER 15

Stop waiting on a sign from God!" Reverend James Bevel's voice boomed from his modest pulpit under the church's single hanging light bulb.

Fannie Lou Hamer's hand stilled. Her paper fan—and the sweltering humidity—were briefly forgotten as she leaned in to hear what the twenty-four-year-old preacher had to say. The church was packed with two hundred people resting their weary bones on hard wooden seats, but it wasn't a Sunday morning, and this wasn't a typical church service.

In this Tuesday night meeting organized by SNCC, Reverend Bevel's goal was to stir fellow Christians to register to vote. "Do not ignore the clear signs [of the times]!" urged the reverend. "God's time is upon us; let us not back down from the challenge [to claim the right to vote now, not later]!"[23]

Hamer felt her spirit stir in response. She estimated that "ninety percent of the Negro people in Mississippi have gone to church all their lives," but she knew they weren't hearing messages like this.[24] For the first time, she was hearing a call to action rather than to patient longsuffering: "Just listenin'… I could see myself votin' people outa office that I know was wrong and didn't do nothin' to help the poor."[25]

To a lifelong Christian like Hamer, Reverend Bevel's injunctions to trust in God *and* roll up one's sleeves to participate in the fight for justice "seemed like the most remarkable thing that could happen in the state of Mississippi."[26]

Bevel and his fellow activists moved from theological exhortation to a more practical explanation of the voter registration process before asking who would be willing to go into Indianola and register.

Hamer's hand shot up in the air. "Had it up as high as I could get," she later recalled.[27]

But this was not a decision made on impulse, and it certainly wasn't made without counting the cost.

"I guess if I'd had any sense I'd a-been a little scared, but what was the point of being scared? The only thing they could do to me was kill me and it seemed like they'd been trying to do that a little bit at a time ever since I could remember," she said of her decision that night.[28]

Due to legal roadblocks and voter intimidation, not a single Black resident of Ruleville had tried to register to vote in the past two years, and only twenty-one had registered in the eight years before that, despite roughly thirteen thousand of them being eligible.

Fear of retribution was only logical. But in Hamer's eyes, the work of Bevel and the SNCC activists was ushering in a "New Kingdom right here on earth." It was a work she wanted to join in, whatever the risk.[29]

But four days later, when Hamer boarded a rented school bus with seventeen other eligible voters for the twenty-five-mile ride to Indianola, Mississippi, she came prepared for the worst. Tucked away in her small bag was a change of clothes and comfortable shoes in case she'd be spending the night in jail.

Everyone's minds were on worst-case scenarios as they rode in near silence to the courthouse. And when they arrived, "most of the people were afraid to get off the bus," recalled one activist. "Then this one little stocky lady just stepped off the bus and went right up to the courthouse and into the clerk's office."[30]

The group filed in silently behind Hamer—though most were sent right back out again. The powers that be insisted the group could only take the registration test two at a time, and the rest would have to wait outside in the hot August sun.

The test was subjective and up to the whims of the county clerk, who demanded Hamer interpret a section of the state constitution on ex post facto laws. "I didn't know nothin' about no de facto laws," Hamer recalled.[31]

By the time she rejoined the group waiting nervously for their turns outside, white supremacists in town were organizing. Many crowded around to harass the group in the light of day. Others waited for the bus to depart for home—which, much to the activists' dismay, was intentionally delayed until dusk.

Highway patrolmen were waiting to pull the bus over as soon as they crossed the bridge out of Indianola. After levying absurd fines for the bus being too yellow and arresting the SNCC leader, the patrolmen eventually allowed the group to continue home.

But citizens picked up where the lawmen left off, with white supremacists in pickup trucks swerving around them, sneering as they brandished their rifles. The tense silence inside the bus was a sharp contrast to their shouted insults—until suddenly, a strong, bold voice arose from within.

> This little light of mine, I'm going to let it shine!
> This little light of mine, I'm going to let it shine!
> This little light of mine, I'm going to let it shine!
> Oh, let it shine, let it shine, let it shine!

Hamer's song rallied the courage of others, and more voices joined in one by one. They sang the rest of the ride home. When Hamer finally arrived back at the plantation, she learned that word traveled faster than the old yellow bus that had carried her back to Ruleville.

Marlow was ready and waiting. He got straight to the point: "I will give you until tomorrow morning. And if you don't withdraw [your voter registration application] you will have to leave."

"I left that same night," said Hamer.[32]

She sheltered with a friend, but nowhere was safe. "They shot in that house sixteen times, tryin' to kill me," she later recalled.[33]

Living like a criminal on the run, Hamer learned that after all these trials, she'd failed the voter registration test anyway. But she'd endured too much to give up now.

"I went back to Indianola to the circuit clerk's office and I told him who I was and I was there to take that…test again," explained Hamer. "I said, 'Now, you cain't have me fired 'cause I'm already fired'…I said, 'I'll be here every thirty days until I become a registered voter.'"

She wouldn't have to prove it. After studying Mississippi's constitution in preparation, Hamer passed the voter registration test on her second attempt.

She had, at last, joined the list of a handful of Black registered voters in Sunflower County—and at the same time, moved right on up the list of targets for white supremacists.

They hadn't been able to stop her. They hadn't been able to kill her. But they were about to make her wish she were dead.

CHAPTER 16

"Please make a way for us, Jesus…where I can stand up and speak for my race and speak for these hungry children."[34]

Fannie Lou Hamer may have been praying out loud, but only God himself could hear her over the racket the storm was making outside. Between the relentless rain pounding on her modest roof and the cracks of thunder shaking the floor beneath her feet, Hamer didn't even hear the man making his way to her front door until a sharp knock interrupted her prayers.

"My name is Charles McLaurin," the visitor shouted over the rain, "and I'm looking for Fannie Lou Hamer!"

Hamer turned in her wingback chair for a better view of the door. "Come in," she shouted back. "I'm Fannie Lou Hamer."

McLaurin opened the door and stomped the mud off his shoes before stepping across the threshold. "Bob Moses told me to come locate you," he said.[35]

Hamer had been in church all her life. As far as she was concerned, when God sends a man named Moses in response to your prayers for freedom, you get up and follow him. Despite the rain coming down in sheets, she left home that very night with a packed bag and a new job title: field secretary for SNCC.

Working for ten dollars a week, Hamer's official responsibility was to organize her community and drive voter registrations. Less officially, she would also serve as a mentor to many of her fellow field secretaries. At forty-five years old, she was the oldest woman in the role and more than twice the average age of her coworkers.

Working alongside young activists that winter, Hamer found inspiration in their bravery. In return, they found comfort in her strength. And as the summer of 1963 arrived, they were all going to need every bit of bravery and strength they could muster.

On the morning of June 9, Hamer watched the sun rise with bleary eyes. She'd been on public buses all night, traveling back to Mississippi from a voter education workshop in Charleston, South Carolina. As the bus rolled to a stop at a bus terminal in Winona, Mississippi, she was more tired than hungry.

When four of her coworkers got off the bus in search of food, Hamer declined to join them. *I'll be home soon enough*, she thought. But a few minutes later, she saw the four young women step back out into the hot sun with empty hands and angry faces.

After climbing off the bus to check on them, Hamer learned that the restaurant in the bus terminal was refusing to serve them. The staff had called in local law enforcement to kick the SNCC workers out. Hamer knew that denying them service was against the law, but she also knew law enforcement in these small towns existed not to enforce the laws so much as the status quo.

"This is what it's like in Mississippi," she told them with a sigh.[36] Rather than make a scene that would only incite violence, Hamer advised her fellow field secretaries to write down the license plate numbers on the squad cars. They could file a report later.

But with every eye in the café peering out the windows, even that proved dangerous. The chief of police and his posse marched outside, grabbed them, and shoved them into the back of the patrol cars.

Despite forty-five years of enduring Mississippi racism, Hamer was shocked. "I didn't go into the bus terminal and I didn't do anything but just got off the bus," she protested from the back seat. "Why was I arrested?"[37]

The officers responded with jeers and racial slurs as they drove past the city jail and right on out to the county jail. Out there, Hamer realized, "They didn't care how loud we hollered, wasn't nobody gon' hear us."[38]

In the booking room, the chief of police stepped forward. "What did you come here for? A demonstration?" Hamer's eyes dropped to the name on his uniform: Herod. "We're gonna teach you a lesson," he growled.[39]

The officers shoved four of the five women into cell blocks, keeping one of the field secretaries, June Johnson, with them. From her cell, Hamer couldn't see what they were doing, but she could certainly hear it. Her stomach turned with the sound of every blow and moan. Johnson, Hamer knew, was only fifteen years old.

Annell Ponder was next. Within ten minutes, the officers had broken her tooth, shattered her cheekbone, and fractured her skull.

Then they came for Hamer.

The officers were tired from their first attacks, but they weren't ready to call it a day. "We gon' make you wish you was dead," said one with a sneer before forcing two Black male prisoners to take over the beatings.[40]

Too terrified to refuse, the prisoners directed Hamer to lie face down on a thin cot in their cell. Hamer tried to shield her body with her hands, but the blows kept coming. When her dress began to slip up, one or more of the officers raped her. "I then began to bury my head in the mattress and hugged it to keep out the sound of my screams. It was impossible to stop screaming," said Hamer.[41]

When the attack finally came to an end, her body was swollen and hard. "When I got back to my cell bed, I couldn't set down. I would *scream*. It hurted me to set down," she recalled.[42]

Despite her own pain and trauma, Hamer was committed to strengthening the young women imprisoned alongside her. Just as she'd done on that first bus ride from Indianola, she began to sing.

> Walk with me, Lord! Walk with me!
> Walk with me, Lord! Walk with me!
> While I'm on, Lord, this pilgrim journey,
> I need Jesus to walk with me.

The other field secretaries listened to Hamer sing and recite Bible verses until their aching bodies slipped into sleep. In too much pain to drift off herself, Hamer was lying awake in the dark when she heard the officers talking in the front room.

"We could put them…in Big Black [River] and nobody would ever find them," they said. They didn't even bother to lower their voices as they discussed ways to make Hamer and her friends disappear forever.[43]

And they probably would have done exactly that if not for the leadership at SNCC contacting Martin Luther King, Jr., who brought national attention to the case before it was too late. After several long days and nights, Hamer and her friends were released.

Limping away from the county jail in the hot summer sun, Hamer was equally sure of two things: By the grace of God, she had come through the valley of the shadow of death. And by the grace of God, she was going to make white supremacists wish they'd killed her when they had the chance.

CHAPTER 17

You can pray until you faint, but if you don't get up and try to do something, God is not going to put it in your lap."[44]

Every eye in the small but packed church was locked on the speaker at the front of the room. The weeknight gathering was much like the one where Reverend Bevel's urge to "stop waiting on a sign from God" had changed Fannie Lou Hamer's life.[45] But this time, the voice ringing out from the podium was her own.

"Jesus said, 'A city that's set on a hill cannot be hid. Let your light so shine that men would see your good works and glorify the Father, which is in Heaven.'…That's why I tell you tonight that you have a responsibility and if you plan to walk in Christ's footstep and keep his commandments you are willing to launch out into the deep and go to the courthouse."

As shouts of "amen" echoed in the pews, Hamer's voice rose to a crescendo: "I believe tonight, that one day in Mississippi—if I have to die for this—we shall overcome."

The small room echoed with the sound of whistles, cheers, stomps, and claps, but Hamer pushed on over the noise: "We have prayed, and we have hoped for God to bring about a change. And now the time have come for people to stand up!"[46]

At this, the audience erupted, ensuring the police waiting outside could hear and feel this movement of God's people.

It had taken a month for the bruises on Hamer's body to fade after the beating she received in jail. In that time, she'd hidden away from her family, protecting them from the trauma of seeing her in such a desperate state. But that would be the last time Hamer hid from anyone.

By the fall, she became a fixture of voting registration events across

Mississippi. With their frequent Scripture references and interpretations, Hamer's speeches carried the weight of a well-crafted sermon.

But as a mere Christian who had scrubbed toilets, picked cotton, faced discrimination, and ultimately survived being beaten within an inch of her life, she was able to bond with her audiences in a way that inspired them to join her.

Once she earned listeners' respect and trust, her call to action was always the same: "We are determined that one day we'll have the power of the ballot. And the sooner you go to the courthouse, the sooner we'll have it."[47]

Hamer and the leaders of SNCC understood that driving Black voter registration—especially in Mississippi—was critical to the cause of social justice nationwide. The white supremacists who had long held political power in the state were unmatched in their commitment to promoting violence, protecting murderers, and ignoring national desegregation laws.

"Mississippi has treated the Negro as if he is a thing instead of a person," observed Martin Luther King, Jr.[48] And that wouldn't change until Black people were able to act on their legal right to vote.

"We want people…over us that's concerned about the people because we are human beings," said Hamer.[49]

But asking people to vote meant asking them to put their lives on the line. After all, a central part of Hamer's story was the discrimination and violence she'd endured for her own participation in the cause. Then, in a stroke of brilliance, the SNCC team devised a way to build momentum while minimizing the immediate risks.

They would hold a mock election that would allow Black Mississippians to experience the voting process without having to pass the incredibly difficult and subjective voter registration test. The results of their election wouldn't stand, of course, but that meant white supremacists would be less concerned about who registered in the first place.

And if people showed up to cast their vote, Mississippi activists would have hard evidence to show the Democratic Party and the nation that there *was* a local interest in voting and that the abysmal registration rates were due to very real threats of retaliation, not disinterest.

Activists, including Hamer, threw themselves headlong into a statewide campaign ahead of their mock election day on November 5, 1963, one year before the next national election. They called it the Freedom Vote.

"This [Freedom Vote] is the most significant fight for freedom in the entire United States," remarked Yale professor Al Lowenstein, "because when you get freedom in Mississippi, we'll have freedom throughout the entire United States."[50]

The results of the vote were staggering. In a state where only twenty thousand of the half a million eligible Black people were registered voters, more than eighty thousand showed up for the unofficial Freedom Vote.

The large turnout energized all the SNCC volunteers for their work to drive real registrations for the 1964 election. "History was being made all over this State this week," declared Bob Moses in the days following the Freedom Vote. "The Negroes do not intend to let another election be held in Mississippi without the Negroes being heard."[51]

Now invigorated by the proof that Black voters would jump at the chance to elect better leaders if their lives weren't in jeopardy, SNCC leaders proposed a radical idea: Fannie Lou Hamer—a Black woman with a sixth-grade education—should run for Congress.

Once again, Charles McLaurin found himself knocking on Hamer's door with an invitation from SNCC. And once again, he drove away with Hamer next to him, ready to go that very night.

This was a woman who was done waiting around for someone else to act.

That summer, Hamer became the first Black woman to run for Congress in the United States, and activists doubled down on their efforts to drive voter registrations—this time, for the real election. They called their campaign Freedom Summer.

Hamer's boldness brought national attention to their efforts, and the cameras that appeared at voter registration rallies ultimately provided some protection for voters.

But the work was still far from safe. Even the state governor announced, "We're going to see that the law is maintained and maintained Mississippi style."[52]

His meaning was soon made clear when, in the first two weeks of Freedom Summer, "there were seven bombings, numerous arrests, five shootings, multiple acts of vandalism, and several beatings," not to mention the abduction and murder of three volunteers.[53]

A storm was raging in Mississippi, and in the eye of that storm was

Mrs. Fannie Lou Hamer, leading volunteers and running a campaign from the shade of a pecan tree in her front yard. As the storm raged on and the threats piled up, Hamer refused to succumb to fear or—even more remarkably—hate.

"The white man [will toss a bomb because he's] afraid he'll be treated like he's been treating the Negroes, but I couldn't carry that much hate," she said. "It wouldn't solve any problems for me to hate whites because they hate me. Oh, there's so much hate! Only God has kept the Negro sane."[54]

Her peace came from a strong assurance that her life and work, no matter how dangerous, were firmly in the center of God's will. "I never know today what's going to happen to me tonight," she admitted, "but I do know as I walk alone, I walk with my hand in God's hand."[55]

And no one could stop the will of God—not even the president of the United States.

CHAPTER 18

For once, the song bubbling up in Fannie Lou Hamer wasn't "This Little Light of Mine" with its stubborn, persistent hope. And it wasn't the mournful plea of "Walk with Me" she'd once sung from the Winona jail.

Standing in the lobby of the 1964 Democratic National Convention after testifying before its Credentials Committee, it was taking everything Hamer had not to burst out in a jubilant rendition of "Go Tell It on the Mountain" right then and there.

Today was a day of promises fulfilled, of a wait that was over. Even the reporters could feel the victory in the air, skirting past Martin Luther King, Jr. to capture one more quote from the woman who'd just captured the hearts of nearly every person in the room.

"I felt just like I was telling it from the mountain!" she told them. "I feel like I'm talking to the world."[56] And when news stations across the country aired her testimony that night, she would be.

The victory wouldn't be official until the next day, when the Credentials Committee gathered to vote on whether to replace delegates from Mississippi's Democratic Party with the sixty-eight delegates put forth by the Mississippi Freedom Democratic Party, including Fannie Lou Hamer herself. Whatever delegates the committee chose would join the national convention that week in nominating the Democratic candidate for president.

Hamer was confident justice would be served. The entire country had just witnessed how the committee members were moved to tears by her story before erupting in a standing ovation.

But power is rarely brokered in front of a camera's blinking red light.

After his desperate White House press conference failed to silence Hamer, President Johnson and his staff went to work calling every member of the

Credentials Committee to threaten anyone leaning toward supporting the MFDP.

Johnson, desperate to unify the Democratic Party around his own name, was terrified his campaign would be as good as dead if he allowed this rogue group of nobodies to unseat Mississippi's all-white delegation.

To the shock of the national media, Johnson's threats worked. When the Credentials Committee took a vote the next day, they failed to deliver the victory Hamer and the MFDP were so certain of. Instead, the committee remained split on which group of delegates to seat, forcing Johnson to send in vice presidential-hopeful Hubert Humphrey to lead both sides to a "compromise"—or, rather, the exact outcome the president himself wanted to see.

The MFDP would be granted two at-large seats, a symbolic gesture with no voting power, while delegates from the Mississippi Democratic Party would be expected to reward Johnson by throwing their unwavering support behind him in the election.

For Humphrey, the mission to broker this compromise was personal—a chance to prove himself and guarantee his spot as Johnson's running mate. So when he met with MFDP representatives behind closed doors, he wasn't too proud to beg.

"Please help us [by agreeing to this compromise]…I'm the best person to be Vice President," Humphrey pleaded to Hamer. "I'm going to work, and the President will work with me for old people, senior citizens, healthcare, education, jobs, and integration, and schools, and all of this."[57]

Hamer was unmoved by the tears in his eyes. "Well, Mr. Humphrey, do you mean to tell me that your position is more important than four hundred thousand Black people's lives?"[58]

Everyone in the room held their breath.

"Mr. Humphrey, if you take this job of Vice President this way, you will never be able to do those things for good, for peace, for old people, for Black people, for colored people, for education. You'll never be able to do it…Senator Humphrey, I'm gonna pray to Jesus for you."[59]

When Hamer marched out of the room, even Martin Luther King, Jr. fell in step behind her.

With the convention now officially underway and the seats for Mississippi's delegates conspicuously empty, Humphrey was running out of time to secure the president's wishes and his own political future.

At the next meeting he organized, Humphrey ensured not a single Mississippian was in the room. He outlined his plan for New Yorker Bob Moses instead: The MFDP would get two nonvoting delegates, and there was no way on earth Fannie Lou Hamer would be one of them.

Moses was incredulous. "You are choosing our delegates? And you're telling us this is freedom?"

But Humphrey was done feigning interest in negotiation. "President Lyndon Johnson told me that 'illiterate woman must never be allowed to speak again at a Democratic convention, and particularly must not have floor privileges to speak,'" he said. "And look at her, the way she dresses, her grammar; this is not the kind of person white America needs to see representing Black people."[60]

The next day, Humphrey insisted, it would be Mississippi's regular, all-white delegates taking their seats on the ballroom floor.

But when Hamer and Moses, still seething, stepped into the balcony to observe the proceedings on Tuesday night, they quickly noticed that only three of Mississippi's dozens of delegate seats were occupied.

The regular delegates were so enraged that the MFDP was given even symbolic at-large seats that most of them boycotted the convention altogether. Johnson's back-door dealings had lost him the support of both groups.

"We didn't come all this way for no two seats," muttered Hamer.[61] Once again, she was the first to step out—and once again, others followed—as she made her way down to the ballroom floor.

One by one, members of the MFDP clasped hands, forming a silent circle on the convention floor as a sign of peaceful protest. The three Mississippi regulars, disgusted by the DNC's refusal to forcefully remove Hamer and friends from the floor, stomped out in a huff.

The next day, the DNC had finally had enough. If Mississippi couldn't get their act together, they'd have no seats at all—literally. When Hamer and her friends arrived that afternoon, the seats for Mississippi's delegates had already been unbolted and removed. Undeterred, they made their way to the gap in the ballroom and sat right down on the hardwood floors.

Almost immediately, security appeared to escort the group out of the building. The door slammed shut behind them with a bang, but Hamer was too numb to flinch.

The fight was over. She had lost. She was leaving Atlantic City with no vote, no voice, and no confidence in her elected leaders.

But work done in the Lord is never in vain. In a foreign land, Fannie Lou Hamer was being lauded as a hero. She just didn't know it yet.

CHAPTER 19

Resting her head on the back of the bathtub, Fannie Lou Hamer let herself close her eyes. It felt as if a lifetime had passed since her days of sneaking into the Marlows' house for a warm bath when no one was home.

Running her hands through the soapy bubbles, she had to admit she'd come a long way from that Mississippi plantation. Who would ever have thought that she, Fannie Lou Hamer, would find herself halfway around the world, relaxing in a beach bungalow on a sprawling estate in Guinea?

The trip had been Harry Belafonte's idea, a way for SNCC leaders to rest and recover after the disappointing end to the 1964 Democratic National Convention. Hamer had never dreamed she would see Africa for herself, but now she was going to tour a country that had recently gained independence from France under the new leadership of President Sekou Touré.

Suddenly, a knock at the door interrupted her thoughts. "Fannie!" called the voice on the other side of the door. "The president is here. Can you come?"

Hamer let out a laugh, "Yeah right! Tell His Excellence that I'll see him in a couple of hours. I'm having my bath, darling."[62]

But the awkward pause on the other side of the door let her know this wasn't a joke. President Touré was waiting. With a gasp, Hamer shot out of the tub and reached for her towel, getting dressed as quickly as she could.

Her hair was still dripping wet when she stepped into the room where Touré was waiting in his stately, all-white attire. He recognized Hamer instantly, moving toward her to offer a kiss on both cheeks. "Africa is your home, and its people your family," he pronounced.[63]

An overwhelmed Hamer burst into tears on Touré's chest.

All her life, she'd been treated as a second-class citizen by the leaders in her country. At almost this very moment, the mayor in Hamer's hometown was telling her neighbors he hoped the Africans would "boil her in tar."[64]

"I've tried so hard so many times to see the president in [my] country and I wasn't given that chance," she later reflected. "But the president over there cared enough to visit us."[65]

Over the next two weeks, Hamer moved in awe through what felt like an upside-down kingdom compared to the land of her childhood.

Some of it was familiar. The women, wearing brightly colored scarves in their hair, singing songs, and carrying pails on their heads, reminded Hamer of her own mother and grandmother.

But unlike Ella Townsend, these women had no need to carry a gun in their buckets. Here, Black people weren't just respected—they were in charge. It filled Hamer with new hope for what might be possible back in Mississippi.

"I saw how the government was run there and I saw where Black people were running [all facets of society]," she said. "It shows what Black people can do if only we get the chance in America. It is there within us. We can do things if we only get the chance."[66]

On the long flight home, Hamer daydreamed about bringing elements of that upside-down kingdom to her own world.

But hope was going to be a difficult thing to hold on to in the days ahead.

Hamer's on-air testimony and congressional campaign had sparked violent backlash from white supremacists across Mississippi. When KKK members heard Hamer was giving a speech at a small, rural church in Benton County a few weeks after her return from Guinea, they showed up just as the last supporters were leaving.

Then they burned the church to the ground.

Some members of the church refused to be intimidated—holding worship services and running a polling station in the open air, right among the charred remains of the building. But others pointed fingers at Hamer. As far as they were concerned, she'd stirred up trouble and brought it right to their front door.

But the primary target was Hamer herself, and she'd just given out her home address on national television. Every night, the phone rang with death threats, and the daytime wasn't much better. On more than one occasion, the very officer who'd terrorized her in the Winona jail drove by slowly, pointing her out to friends in his pickup truck.

On Election Day, Fannie Lou Hamer made history as the MFDP's candidate for Congress, her name stamped proudly on official ballots across the state. But with fewer than 5 percent of eligible Black voters actually registered, SNCC leaders knew Hamer couldn't win.

After her loss was certified, Hamer filed a challenge, claiming the official results were unconstitutional "because Negroes throughout the State of Mississippi...were systematically and almost totally excluded from the electoral process."[67]

Her argument garnered enough support to earn her a hearing before the House of Representatives in Washington. At the hearing, Hamer made history yet again, this time as the first Black woman to be seated on the floor of the House of Representatives.

"When we go back home from this meeting here today, we stand a chance of being shot down, or either blown to bits in the state of Mississippi," she testified to the House committee. "I might not live two hours after I get back home, but I want to be part of helping set the Negro free in Mississippi."[68]

Hamer and the MFDP did everything humanly possible to win the challenge, but the House ultimately voted to dismiss them. After the vote, Hamer wept openly on the steps of the Capitol building.

"I'm not crying for myself alone," she told reporters. "I'm crying for America. Because it is later than you think."[69]

Hamer was emotionally and physically exhausted. "I don't feel well at all," she confessed to a friend. "My kidneys are giving me trouble, and my head, too."[70]

Back home, her twenty-four-year-old daughter, Dorothy, was struggling with her own health complications during a difficult pregnancy. Hamer decided to step out of the spotlight for a while to better support her: "I am going to do all I can for her and the baby. I have been away from my family so much, and now they need all my help."[71]

The birth came and went without major issues, but Dorothy's health continued to deteriorate. Then, on May 24, 1967, Dorothy suffered a cerebral hemorrhage and fell into a coma as Hamer raced her to the hospital. Hamer stayed up all night praying by her bedside, but the next morning, her daughter was gone.

Devastated, Hamer mentally replayed the events of the past few years on repeat. If she'd gotten Dorothy to the hospital sooner, if she'd done things differently, if, if, if…could things have turned out better?

Despite her sacrifices, she'd faced failure after failure professionally and personally. She had glimpsed the hope of a better kingdom, but she still longed to see the goodness of the Lord in the land of the living—in *her* land.

And by God's grace, she soon would.

CHAPTER 20

The 1968 Democratic National Convention started much like the one four years prior. But this time, when Fannie Lou Hamer stepped onto the convention floor, it wouldn't be as a protester. It would be as a hero.

Once again, the convention began with a hearing before the Credentials Committee where the MFDP, now in partnership with other groups, argued that their diverse delegation was a more just representation of the people of Mississippi.

Once again, the all-white group of regular delegates threatened to support the Republican nominee for president if they were forced to share seats with these protesters.

And once again, the Credentials Committee heard testimonies much like those given in 1964 before proposing a compromise to share the seats, a proposal that the MFDP rejected.

But this time, after three days of deliberation, the committee voted to oust every single one of Mississippi's regular delegates and to seat all of the challengers in their place. Fannie Lou Hamer would be the first female delegate from Mississippi and the Democratic Party's first Black delegate since the post–Civil War Reconstruction period.

And she wouldn't be the last.

When Fannie Lou Hamer walked out and took her seat on the convention floor, the room erupted in a standing ovation. Glowing with joy, Hamer peered around the room. What she saw was a direct result of her fervent prayers and years of sacrifice: signs of change.

Just four years ago, Hamer and her friends had been escorted out of the convention by security. But now, a record-breaking 340 Black delegates and alternates from across the United States were among those applauding Hamer across the convention floor.

And the changes extended beyond the four walls of that room. In the 1968 elections, 108 Black Americans ran for office in state primaries. Of those, thirty-two would move on to the general election in November, and six—including two personal friends of Hamer—would ultimately win their races.

That's not to say the fight for civil rights had gotten any safer.

Just two months before the convention, Bobby Kennedy, the presidential hopeful backed by many civil rights activists, was shot and killed within hours of winning the Democratic primary in California. Two months before that, Martin Luther King, Jr. was assassinated on a motel balcony in Memphis, Tennessee.

And two years after the convention, another attempt was made on Hamer's life, but the pipe bomb tossed in her front yard failed to explode.

Unfortunately, the ticking time bomb within her own body wouldn't be so easy to defuse.

In the early 1970s, Hamer struggled with her mental and physical health, due in part to the lingering effects of the abuse she'd endured in Winona. While her repeated hospital stays forced her to slow down, she remained committed to serving her community.

Even after an unsuccessful run for state senate in 1971, Hamer never stopped working to drive voter registrations, fight for desegregation, and care for every single impoverished person who knocked on her front door.

"She didn't turn them down," her family observed. "She would give her *last*."[72]

Then, in 1976, she received a diagnosis from which she wouldn't recover: breast cancer. Despite a mastectomy, the once-formidable Hamer quickly grew weak and dependent on her family.

But she also experienced what she'd once read Paul describe in his letter to the Corinthians. Her body was wasting away, but her spirit was being renewed day by day as God allowed her to glimpse a glory that would far outweigh her temporary troubles (see 2 Corinthians 4:16-18).

Financial support, awards, and certificates of recognition poured in as people sought to let Hamer know what a difference her work had made.

On November 1, 1976, the mayor of Ruleville—sitting in an office once held by a man who wished to see Hamer burned in tar—declared it Fannie Lou Hamer Day. The celebration that ensued was but a shadow of the glory yet to come.

Four months later, on March 14, 1977, fifty-nine-year-old Fannie Lou Hamer stepped into that glory at last.

The following Sunday, her close family and friends, including some of the nation's leading civil rights leaders, gathered inside Williams Chapel Baptist Church for her funeral. Nearly 1,500 more supporters gathered on the lawn outside to hear the eulogies delivered over portable speakers.

"None of us would be where we are today had she not been here then." The voice booming across the crowd belonged to Andrew Young, Georgia's first Black congressman since Reconstruction who had recently been appointed US ambassador to the United Nations.

"She was despised…tormented by suffering…yet on herself she bore our suffering…Little did we realize that here amongst us was one of God's chosen, who would change the lives of us all."[73]

Turning his attention to the gold-trimmed coffin at the front of the church, Young then spoke for not only everyone listening that day but also countless Mississippians, Black Americans, and mere Christians to come: "Thank you for your inspiration, and thank you for the example. Thank you for soul strengthening our lives, so that we might live so that God can use us anytime and anywhere. This little light of mine, I'm gonna let it shine."[74]

THREE WAYS TO GLORIFY GOD IN YOUR WORK AS SEEN IN THE LIFE OF FANNIE LOU HAMER

I (Jordan) have never met a Black friend who doesn't know Fannie Lou Hamer's story. And I have never met a white friend who does. That's tragic because, regardless of your race, Hamer offers a remarkable case study on how you can glorify God whether you're an activist, an architect, or an astronomer. I'm sure you picked up nuggets to that end throughout the biography. But allow me to be explicit here about what we can learn from Fannie Lou Hamer about honoring the Lord at work.

I. MERE CHRISTIANS GLORIFY GOD BY DOING JUSTICE WITHOUT HATING THE UNJUST.

All throughout Scripture, we see the "God of justice" (Isaiah 30:18) calling his people to pursue justice on his behalf—perhaps most memorably in the Great Requirement of Micah 6:8, which compels you and me "to act justly and to love mercy and to walk humbly with [our] God."

The world often tells us that doing justice requires that we also publicly shame and "cancel" the unjust. But God calls his people to a different way— glorifying him by pursuing justice while refusing to hate the perpetrators of injustice.

That is what Christ called us to in the Sermon on the Mount (see Matthew 5:43-44) and what he himself demonstrated on the mount of Calvary where he used some of his final painful breaths to pray that God would forgive his enemies.

Fannie Lou Hamer offers us a case study of what it looks like to reflect our Savior in this way today. She boldly confronted the injustices of her time, and yet, in the words of one of her biographers, "she faced her enemies with amazing grace and forgiveness."[75] Hamer said, "You can't love God and hate," and she practiced what she preached.[76]

What will it look like practically for you, like Fannie Lou Hamer, to do justice without hating the unjust today?

First, *take a risk to speak out against injustice.* Do you see a coworker being treated unfairly by your boss? Have you noticed discrimination in pay or promotions? As God's ambassador in your place of work, you are called to speak out against these injustices respectfully (see Ephesians 5:11). This, of course, is risky. But this is the way of Jesus exemplified by Fannie Lou Hamer, who consistently put herself in harm's way as a means of loving her neighbor as herself.

Second, *refuse to take revenge against the unjust.* Romans 12:19 says, "Do not take revenge...but leave room for God's wrath." Hamer lived out this command particularly in the way she dealt with her unjust and unfaithful husband, Pap. The press frequently asked Hamer about her husband, giving her plenty of opportunities to destroy his reputation. But "she never publicly spoke" of his many affairs.[77]

Finally, if you want to glorify God at work today, *pray for the unjust.* When Fannie Lou Hamer was being pushed around by the next vice president of the United States, she not only refused to hate him but also *prayed* for him. Jesus said, "Love your enemies and pray for those who persecute you" (Matthew 5:44). Who is *your* enemy today? Pray for them, knowing that you are glorifying your Father in heaven as you do.

2. MERE CHRISTIANS GLORIFY GOD BY TRUSTING IN GOD AND HUSTLING IN THEIR WORK.

There's a tension we see throughout Scripture. On the one hand, we are told to trust in God as "it is he who gives you the ability to produce wealth" and have any sort of impact in your work (see Deuteronomy 8:17-18). On the other hand, we are told to hustle and "work heartily, as for the Lord" (see Colossians 3:23, ESV).

So which is it? Are we called to trust, or are we called to hustle? The answer is both. Mere Christians glorify God by embracing the tension between trusting in God *and* hustling in the work God has called us to do.

Fannie Lou Hamer held this tension well—but not at first. She spent years *only* trusting and waiting on a "sign from God."[78] But everything changed for Hamer when she heard Reverend Bevel issue "a call to action rather than to patient longsuffering." A call not to let go and let God but to trust God and get going, joining him where he was clearly moving to end injustice in Mississippi.

Hamer summed up this principle perfectly when she said, "You can pray until you faint, but if you don't get up and try to do something, God is not going to put it in your lap."[79]

Take a moment right now to think of a project you've already begun or feel God might be calling you to start. It doesn't have to be something as dramatic as Hamer's campaign for voting rights. It could simply be a goal to grow your business in order to serve more people. Here's how you, like Hamer, can embrace the tension between trusting and hustling.

First, *pray and communicate your trust in the Lord for the results of this project.* Humbly recognize that apart from him you can do nothing of eternal consequence (see John 15:5).

Second, *define a single next action you can take to "get going."* After hearing Reverend Bevel's sermon, Hamer knew her next action was to raise her hand and volunteer to register to vote.

Finally, *commit to regularly resting from your work.* In doing so, you will be demonstrating your reliance on God for the results in your work, thus glorifying him.

3. MERE CHRISTIANS GLORIFY GOD BY BELIEVING THAT GOD IS CREATING AN IMPACT THROUGH THEIR WORK EVEN WHEN THAT WORK APPEARS TO BE IN VAIN.

First Corinthians 15:58 promises that "your labor in the Lord is not in vain," meaning that while any work you do for *your* fame, for *your* fortune, and according to *your* rules will perish, any work you do for *God's* glory, powered by *God's* Spirit, and according to *God's* rules will last for eternity—even if that work appears to be "in vain" today.

Again, the life of Fannie Lou Hamer illustrates this truth beautifully. The first time I read about the 1964 Democratic National Convention—Hamer's riveting testimony, the standing ovation from the Credentials Committee, and the response of the national press—I was *certain* Fannie Lou Hamer and the MFDP would be victorious.

When I learned that they failed, it felt like a punch to the gut. I can only imagine how it felt for Hamer. Nobody could blame her if she viewed her activism as "vanity of vanities" (Ecclesiastes 1:2-3, ESV).

But God knew something that Hamer couldn't. He knew that he would use her failure to soften the ground for victory in 1968. He also knew that at the same time her work of doing justice was reviled in America, it was being celebrated in the distant land of Guinea.

There's a principle embedded in that for you, believer. Even when you experience failure and setbacks in your work, so long as that work is done for God's glory and the good of others, it will *always* have an impact in the seemingly distant land God calls the kingdom of heaven.

What are you working on that feels as if it has been in vain? Maybe it's a product you're launching that isn't gaining traction. Maybe it's a coworker you've been faithfully sharing the gospel with who seems to have zero interest in Christ. Or maybe it's an injustice in your industry that you can't seem to overcome.

Romans 4:20-21 says that Abraham "gave glory to God," simply by having faith that God would "do what he had promised." God has promised that if your work is "in the Lord"—if you are launching that product, sharing the gospel, or fighting injustice for God's glory and the good of others—then it "*is not in vain*" (1 Corinthians 15:58). And you can glorify God simply by having faith in that promise today!

PART III

OLE KIRK CHRISTIANSEN

FOUNDER OF LEGO

HOW TO GLORIFY GOD BY PERSEVERING THROUGH ADVERSITY,
EMBRACING "USELESS" WORK, AND MASTERING YOUR CRAFT

CHAPTER 21

F ire! Fire!"

The muffled pounding of fists on his door downstairs and frantic shouts from his employees outside woke a deeply sleeping Ole Kirk Christiansen in an instant. He reached for a light switch but to no avail—a snowstorm had downed the power lines while he slept.

After rushing down the stairs in the dark, Christiansen stumbled out into the night, hardly registering the bitter cold of snow and ice as he drew near to the fiery furnace of his workshop. Someone tried calling for help, only to find local telephone lines had already suffered the same wintry fate as the power lines.

Fortunately, word spreads fast in a small town, and in 1942, Billund, Denmark, was a *very* small town. Local men and boys raced to the scene with buckets and rudimentary firefighting equipment to help their friend. Working together, the community eventually got the blaze under control while Christiansen's wife and young daughter watched wide-eyed from across the street.

When the sun finally rose, sympathetic neighbors and shocked employees gathered to take in the spectacle. Stunned by the depths of devastation, Christiansen retreated to his bedroom and dropped to his knees.

The building that had just gone up in flames was the LEGO factory. Still decades from becoming the global powerhouse we know today, the bustling workshop employed a few dozen Billund residents to create wooden toys. But all that was left of it now was a smoldering heap.

The fire had mercilessly laid claim to everything in Christiansen's shop. The losses—from melted machinery to unshipped customer orders—far exceeded the company's insurance policy.

It would be a devastating blow even in the best of times, and 1942 was far from the best of times. Nazi Germany had invaded Denmark two years prior.

Even food and basic commodities were hard to come by, much less the tools and resources needed to rebuild a toy factory.

Lying prostrate on his bedroom floor, Christiansen cried out to God. What happened next so surprised the overwhelmed business owner that he quickly recorded it in his personal journal: "I experienced something remarkable: the prayer became a thanks and a blessing for me. I was given invisible help. It was as though my difficulties were taken from me."[1]

He stood up, went downstairs, and gathered his family and employees for a group photo in front of the charred remains of his workshop. He would never know what caused the devastating fire, but he was determined to mark this moment. He trusted that it wasn't the end of the LEGO story but rather an opportunity for God to be glorified.

Then he got to work.

That very day, Christiansen helped his team search through the rubble for any salvageable toys that could be sold as a first step to recouping his losses. And over the coming months, he accrued the materials he needed to rebuild his factory.

When construction finally began that summer, Christiansen returned to his journal to submit his plans to the Lord, writing, "We have come to the result that without him we can do nothing…My prayer to the Lord for LEGO is that he will help us run a business that is honest in every way…so that our actions and our lives are lived in his honor."[2]

At the height of World War II, Christiansen watched his factory burn to the ground, bringing him to the brink of bankruptcy—and yet, within months, he was cheerfully rebuilding and looking forward with hope to the future of the company. How?

As you'll see throughout his story, Christiansen didn't rely on positive self-talk, the latest business books, or his own ability to hustle hard enough to turn things around. He had a deeply rooted faith in God, with full confidence that his heavenly Father loved him and had a plan for LEGO.

Christiansen never went to seminary or traveled to foreign countries as a missionary. Instead, he walked with God daily right where he was called: as a mere Christian running a small-town business in rural Denmark.

But that calling was far from easy. Over his lifetime, Christiansen witnessed his workshop burn to the ground and then set about rebuilding it in faith—not once but *three* separate times. And as you'll soon see, those fires were far from the most dramatic setbacks he faced.

The following story is filled with a nearly unbelievable series of hardships—from Nazi occupation to personal loss—that drove the LEGO founder to his knees time and time again. And time and time again, Christiansen rose from his desperate prayers with renewed confidence that God would work everything for good.

But Christiansen's story isn't just engrossing. It is also terrifically enlightening. It's a narrative that shows how mere Christians like you can glorify God by persevering through trials, embracing play and work the world deems useless, and committing yourself to the ministry of excellence as a means of loving your neighbor as yourself.

Few people know the story of Ole Kirk Christiansen, but once you do, you'll never look at a pile of shiny LEGOs—or your own work—the same way again.

CHAPTER 22

Ole Kirk Christiansen was not yet six years old when he created his first toy. The hands that would one day mold plastic into the world's most popular plaything started with much simpler materials: a stone and some string.

Where others might see an ordinary rock, young Ole Kirk saw potential. After threading a string through a hole in the stone, he pulled the rock behind him everywhere he went. In his vivid imagination, it was now a beloved pet cow following him around the family farm.

Born into a community of poor farmers in rural Denmark in 1891, Ole Kirk had a humble but happy childhood. Most days, he helped look after the family's sheep and cows, usually with his toy cow tethered to a nearby post. He learned to read and write while attending school two days a week, played and sang with his twelve siblings, and learned from his hardworking parents that God was merciful and trustworthy.

Even as a child, Ole Kirk demonstrated a commitment to excellence in his work. Much like a young King David protecting the family's flock, the boy shepherd kept a sharp eye out for dangerous clay pits, venomous snakes, and ominous storm clouds.

At the age of fourteen, he traded the childhood work of one biblical king for another. Like Jesus of Nazareth, Ole Kirk spent his teen years apprenticing as a carpenter alongside family.

Over time, he became a journeyman carpenter with dreams of settling down and setting up his own shop. Just shy of his twenty-fifth birthday, he got the chance he'd been looking for when a single-story home and workshop went up for sale in Billund, a small village of about a hundred people not far from where he grew up.

The home was on the outskirts of town, at the very end of a long gravel road. Beyond it was nothing but an endless expanse of fields and open skies.

With loans from his siblings and the bank, Ole Kirk purchased the unassuming property in 1915. He marked the happy occasion with two new names. The first, of course, was for his fledgling business, which he called Billund Woodworking & Carpentry (a respectable name for a respectable business with absolutely no plans to produce toys of any kind).

The second name, oddly enough, was for himself. He was born Ole Kirk *Kristiansen*, with a K, but from this moment onward, he would spell his last name *Christiansen*. His descendants have differed on which spelling they prefer, but once Ole Kirk opted to identify with Christ in name, he took that name to his grave.

Like many young adults, Christiansen found his twenties to be a whirlwind. Within two years of purchasing his workshop, he moved in, made Hansine Kristine Sørensen his wife, and became the proud father of his firstborn son.

The young family found a local faith community through the Inner Mission, an evangelical organization whose members had a reputation for being stern and deeply committed to their beliefs. Christiansen himself was certainly steadfast in his convictions, but no one ever accused him of being straitlaced. On the contrary, the young carpenter was known to be a practical jokester, full of joy and prone to playfulness.

He also quickly built a reputation as a masterful carpenter, and before long, he had enough demand to hire a handful of employees from the local area and beyond. Employees were treated as part of the family, gathering together for meals where Christiansen led them in prayer, hymns, and devotional readings.

But the boss's faith wasn't just one of lip service around the dinner table. It influenced every aspect of his work, which he saw as an opportunity to serve others.

One example comes from his relationship with a young orphan he employed as an apprentice. Business owners of the time typically did not pay apprentices any wages beyond free room and board. But Christiansen coached the boy on how to make extra income by working with company tools after hours and gathering wood shavings from the workshop to sell as kindling. He never once asked for a share in the profits.

Christiansen's carpentry business grew, and so did his family. By 1920, the couple had welcomed three sons in four years. (Their fourth and final boy followed six years later.) Godtfred, the third-born son who would one day take over the family business, described his dad's motto in just three words: "Pray and work."[3]

It was a simple motto, and the quiet house on the edge of town was the perfect setting for a simple life. But there was more on the horizon than what Christiansen could see down that long gravel road. Business wasn't going to stay simple for very long.

CHAPTER 23

There was a chill in the air as Ole Kirk Christiansen's young apprentice swung his leg over the bicycle, and then checked again to ensure the envelope of cash was tucked safely inside his pocket. If that money didn't reach the bank by 3:00, the carpenter would lose both the workshop and his home.

Despite the high stakes, Christiansen masked any anxiety with a warm smile and kind word as the teenager set off on a sixteen-mile round trip to the bank, gravel crunching under his tires. As the bike disappeared down the road, Christiansen turned back to the workshop with a sigh.

In the first few years of Billund Woodworking & Carpentry, Denmark's neutrality in World War I meant business was booming for the nation's farmers. With a steady stream of income, Christiansen's neighbors had money to spare on equipment repairs, new barns, and plenty of other projects that kept him busy.

But then World War I gave way to a global financial crisis—a new kind of battle that no country could elect to sit out. Suddenly, farmers quit calling on Christiansen for his services. And when they did need to hire him, they always asked to barter or purchase on credit.

Before long, it seemed as if every knock at the door announced the arrival of another debt collector rather than a paying customer. Despite the frequency of his apprentice's eleventh-hour bike rides to the bank, Christiansen remained determined to grow his business and keep his staff.

Conventional wisdom would call for reduced spending in a recession, but ever the relentless optimist, Christiansen invested in expansion instead. He built on to his workshop, adding rooms he could rent out for additional income.

Then one cold April day in 1924, not long after the project was complete, everyone settled down for a Sunday nap. Well, almost everyone. Four-year-old

Godtfred and five-year-old Karl Georg waited until the house was quiet before sneaking downstairs to play in the workshop.

The boys wanted to build dollhouse furniture for the girls next door, but the cold was making their fingers stiff. Not to be deterred by a little thing like freezing temperatures, the boys struck a match to light the oven, just as they'd seen their father do a thousand times. But this time, a spark leaped from the oven and landed on the dry wood shavings scattered across the workshop floor.

As the boys soon discovered, nothing catches fire faster than a carpenter's workshop. There was smoke. There was shouting. Christiansen and his wife sprang from the bed, racing to find their young sons.

Miraculously, everyone made it safely outside. Christiansen's faithful apprentice had broken through the workshop's locked door to rescue the boys just in time. But the little white house, the workshop, the newly built apartment—all of it burned to the ground in no time at all.

Christiansen was in shock. Everything he'd built was gone, leaving him with a mountain of debt and no insurance policy to cover his losses.

Still deeply convinced of God's goodness, Christiansen didn't grieve long. Almost immediately, he began sketching out a plan for a bigger and better workshop; then he called upon a talented architect to make his vision a reality.

The cold spring was just giving way to summer when the foundation was laid for Christiansen's new home and business. As the building took shape, the neighbors began to talk. How could the debt-ridden carpenter afford a home like *that* in times like *these*?

Truth be told, Christiansen couldn't afford it, but he was never one to do anything halfway. Within months, his impressive brick home was the largest in town. Wide windows framed a storefront display, and in a final extravagant flourish, a pair of imposing stone lions flanked the front door.

The family had barely settled in before lightning struck the newly built workshop in 1926. Just two years after the first fire, the workshop burned to the ground once more. (This time, the family home was mercifully unscathed.)

Most people might consider a lightning strike from the heavens a sign to stop, but it was clear by this point that Ole Kirk Christiansen was not like most people. Just as he did after the first fire in 1924 and the third fire in 1942, Christiansen took his worries to God, and then set about rebuilding his business.

Within a few years, things started looking up at last. An exceptionally good harvest in 1928 meant farmers had money to spend, so Christiansen did too. He even purchased one of the area's first automobiles and was soon bouncing around from job to job in a Model T.

But all too soon, a rush on Wall Street nearly four thousand miles away plunged the world into another economic crisis, and debt collectors resumed their knocking at Christiansen's front door.

In an effort to love his neighbor as himself, Christiansen put off as long as possible asking his hard-pressed customers for the money they owed him. But when the lumberyard finally refused to extend any more wood on credit, he had no other choice. Without wood, how could he work? How could he shelter and feed his family? What would happen to his employees?

Out of options and out of time, Christiansen climbed into his Model T and set out. It was a long day of whispered apologies and closed doors. The only customer even willing to sign a promissory note for the money they owed was the local butcher at his very last stop—and that was only after Christiansen promised to lend his own money if the butcher found himself in need.

Praying for a way to keep his business afloat a little longer, Christiansen was sweeping the mostly empty workshop when yet another foreboding knock came at the front door. The person on the other side was about to change everything.

CHAPTER 24

Ole Kirk Christiansen took a deep breath and went to the door, already thinking through what he could say to pacify yet another debt collector. The last time the bailiff had shown up to confront the carpenter about unpaid debts, Christiansen had bought some time by gifting him with a haul of handcrafted items for his family. Perhaps that would work again?

Fortunately, he wouldn't have to find out. For once, the face on the other side of the door was a friendly one. It belonged to a lumber merchant known as "Wood" Olesen.

Relieved, Christiansen welcomed his friend inside to warm up by the workshop's oven and enjoy a cup of coffee. As the two began talking, Olesen revealed that many of the carpentry businesses he served were closing up shop. He'd come to see what Billund Woodworking & Carpentry was doing to avoid the same fate.

Christiansen, who hadn't been hired for a large job in months, explained that he was mostly building small household items he hoped would sell, even in a recession. Olesen ran his hands over ladders and ironing boards, admiring their workmanship as he listened. But when a shelf of gleaming toy cars caught his attention from across the room, he pivoted at once to get a closer look.

As he picked up a shiny red model and gave the wooden wheels a gentle spin, it was easy to see the wheels in his head turning just as quickly.

Olesen began thinking out loud, outlining a plan that just might save both their businesses: If Christiansen could complete a large order of toy cars over the summer, then Olesen could take them to shopkeepers around the region in the fall, just in time for Christmas gift shopping. The lumber merchant, who always kept a close eye on trends in Danish craftsmanship, was confident that wooden toys like these were on the way in.

Christiansen was intrigued. Up until this point, he had only made the toys because he enjoyed the process and delighted in watching his children play with them. But Olesen's excitement was contagious. Could this be the answer to his prayers? Could the toys actually generate enough income to keep his floundering business afloat?

After waving goodbye to his friend, Christiansen turned to Kristine, who could see the shiny gleam of hope in his eyes. At first, he tried to stay casual about the plan. "This might be the way to go, eh?" he asked her. "We can always dip our toes into the water with a couple of…wooden cars and some other toys."[4]

But then, Christiansen had never been one to dip his toes into anything. Diving into the deep end was more his style. Before long, neighbors noticed the sign in front of the carpenter's workshop boasted a new name: O. Kirk Christiansen's Woodwork & Toy Factory. He was going all in.

As word spread around town, it quickly became clear that not everyone thought the idea was a good one. His friends at the Inner Mission were a pious group known for taking themselves quite seriously. They couldn't imagine why a well-respected carpenter like Christiansen would spend his days creating children's playthings.

Even his older siblings pushed back on the idea. "I think you're much too good for that, Christiansen," they told him outright. "Why don't you find something more useful to do!"[5]

After watching their brother become a master carpenter, they couldn't believe he was returning to the hobbies of his boyhood, whittling wooden toys and creating pull-behind animals such as his old stone "cow."

Their questioning glances and dismissive remarks did nothing to squelch their brother's growing excitement. Christiansen believed that play was inherently good for children—and adults too, for that matter. It wasn't uncommon for his employees to find him knocking at their front door on a Sunday afternoon, inviting them and their families to come outside and join his family in a game.

In 1932, child psychologists were just starting to understand the educational benefits of play. Christiansen's love of quality toys—and his hope that fellow parents would buy them during hard times—was largely based on instinct and his own personality. But just as he began production on his first order of wooden cars, a new toy was taking the world by storm: yo-yos.

Yo-yos were a simple toy that most families could afford even amid the Great Depression. They gave children and adults alike a welcome distraction from the hardships that surrounded them. And their sudden popularity suggested that maybe building a toy company wasn't so crazy after all.

With the help of his family and a few local employees, Christiansen moved quickly to produce and ship thousands of the sought-after toy to distributors across Denmark. With yo-yo orders flying out the doors and Olesen's toy cars filling the workshop shelves, Billund's little toy business was bustling with energy from early in the morning until late at night.

With each passing day, Christiansen grew more confident that this new venture could glorify God and provide for his family—and not a moment too soon. Kristine was pregnant again.

As summer gave way to the first days of fall, the carpenter was brimming with the joy of new life in both his home and his business.

He never could have imagined he was on the brink of his darkest season yet.

CHAPTER 25

A jumbled flurry of musical scales filled the front room of the Christiansen home. Twelve-year-old Godtfred was playing around on the family organ when he felt a heavy hand on his shoulder. He looked up to find his father staring into space, the usual gleam in his eyes shrouded in a veil of shock and confusion.

Godtfred's hands fell away from the keys, the sudden silence somehow louder than the chaotic chords from moments before.

Christiansen took a seat and a deep breath. His words tumbled out in fits and starts as he tried to do the impossible: to explain something he didn't understand himself, to console his son with a comfort he didn't feel.

It had all happened so fast. A few days prior, a heavily pregnant Kristine had remarked that she wasn't feeling well. Most days of her fifth pregnancy had been difficult, but this was different. This was worse.

They rushed to the hospital in Grindsted, only to find out there was nothing that could be done. Their unborn child's heart was no longer beating.

Kristine gave birth to their stillborn child, enduring the pains of labor without the promise of joy on the other side. In the grief-filled hours that followed, there was a glimmer of hope: It seemed Kristine was going to heal physically, even if her heart would take much longer to mend.

Then, without warning, Kristine was gone too. Stunned by the loss of his child and wife in the span of just days, Christiansen struggled to comprehend the words of the sympathetic doctor: "A blood clot...Nothing we could do...I'm so sorry."

Back at home with his young son, Christiansen's bewildered voice gave way to sobs. It was the first time Godtfred had ever seen his father cry, and he'd never forget it. Together, they knelt to pray before they rose to break the heartbreaking news to Godtfred's brothers.

Trusting firmly in the promise of resurrection, Christiansen knew that he would one day be reunited with Kristine in the presence of Jesus (see 1 Thessalonians 4:13-14). But that distant hope was only a partial comfort in the raw grief of sudden loss.

Years later, Christiansen would sit at his typewriter and remember, "I tried to say, 'Thy will be done, Lord Jesus,' and to truly live it, but remained sickened by grief."[6]

The void left by Kristine was immense. Her heartbroken widower was suddenly faced with the daunting prospect of raising four grieving boys, managing a household, and leading his business down an entirely new path—a path that, despite his early optimism, seemed destined to end in failure.

Inside O. Kirk Christiansen's Woodwork & Toy Factory, inventory shelves were crowded with toys from Wood Olesen's large order that had inspired the recent rebrand. But days passed, then weeks, and the lumber merchant still hadn't come for his order.

Eventually, word reached Christiansen that his friend had gone bankrupt. With no money to buy the toys he'd ordered, Olesen wouldn't be coming to pick them up. Limbs heavy with grief, Christiansen stacked the canceled order into his Model T. He'd have to carry out his friend's plan on his own.

Olesen had been sure shop owners would jump at the chance to stock their shelves with the high-quality toys, but Christiansen's day as a door-to-door salesman did nothing to restore his faith in the future of his company. He slashed prices to offload what he could and then returned home, just relieved the day was over.

The relief was short-lived. Waiting for him back at the workshop were thousands of meticulously crafted yo-yos and no buyers in sight. The fad that had inspired so much excitement a few months before was already over. And with Christmas just a few weeks away, it was already clear that holiday shopping alone wasn't going to be enough to save the company.

Desperate to offload the rest of his inventory, the toymaker placed an ad in the newspaper. If anyone was interested in one thousand or more yo-yos, he'd guarantee the cheapest price around and deliver them immediately.

As 1932 turned to 1933, a grieving Christiansen prayed often—for his business, for his boys, and for a path out of the darkest valley he'd ever known. But hope still felt out of reach.

"To be honest, I've given up," he told one lawyer who came knocking on his door. "I owe debts everywhere, my wife is dead, and I'm left with four children who depend on me. What am I supposed to do? I might as well pack it in right now."[7]

Late one night, painfully aware of the empty space in the bed beside him, Christiansen tossed and turned, taking his fears to God in fitful prayers. *Are they right, God? Was this all a big mistake? Is this the end of the road for my business?*

He didn't really expect an answer from the heavens at that very moment, but by the grace of God, that's exactly what he got.

CHAPTER 26

Lying in the dark, Ole Kirk Christiansen's anxious thoughts swirled rapidly in circles above his head. But as he prayed, the chaos calmed, and a crystal-clear vision came into focus in its place. "I saw a large factory where busy people were bustling in and out, where raw materials were brought in and finished goods dispatched," he explained.[8]

He wasn't manifesting the future he wanted or convincing himself to simply try harder. Rather, he felt his heart, mind, and body relax with a sudden peace that could only come from the One who knows what the future holds.

"The image was so clear that I never again doubted I would one day reach my goal: it was the factory that today is a reality," Christiansen later recalled. "I'm certain that it's God who gives us visions like that."[9]

The next morning, Christiansen awoke with a renewed heart, ready to walk hand in hand with God through the messiness of his current circumstances. He would start, he decided, by getting his home in order. In October 1933, Christiansen placed an ad looking for a woman who could manage the work once done by Kristine: cooking, managing the household, and taking care of his boys.

Over a hundred miles away, thirty-seven-year-old Sofie Jørgensen was dealing with her own disappointments. Unlike most of her friends, Sofie had never married. Without children of her own to raise, she'd spent the last several years working in a home for troubled boys. Week after week, she set aside part of her paycheck as seed money for her dream: running a business of her own.

Then she heard about a job opening for a store manager in her hometown of Haslev. The role sounded perfect for an aspiring entrepreneur like Sofie. She traveled home to apply for the position, but her rising hopes were quickly dashed when she wasn't offered the role.

Deeply saddened by the rejection, Sofie stopped by a friend's house for coffee and company. It was there that Christiansen's ad in a newspaper on the table caught her eye. With no other prospects on the horizon, Sofie replied to the ad. The answer came quickly. The job was hers.

Setting aside her dreams of running her own business, Sofie set out for Billund. She had no way of knowing God was about to use her backup plan to give her the deepest desires of her heart.

When Sofie arrived, the Christiansen boys took to her almost instantly. To everyone's surprise, so did their dad. A whirlwind romance ensued, and just seven months after answering his ad, Sofie became Mrs. Ole Kirk Christiansen.

In Billund, Sofie not only found love but also an opportunity to help run a business, just as she'd dreamed. The money she'd saved up for just that purpose saved O. Kirk Christiansen's Woodwork & Toy Factory from bankruptcy.

As for her new husband, Sofie's presence filled him with fresh hope for his family and his venture. In 1935, a reinvigorated Christiansen set out for a trade fair in Fredericia to look for trends and opportunities in the toy industry. What he saw convinced him that first and foremost, his business needed a new brand.

When he returned home, he landed on the name that has been stamped on billions of toys ever since: LEGO. Superfans may know that LEGO in Latin means "I gather," a fitting description for the process of playing with the popular bricks. But that was a happy accident the Christiansens didn't discover for years. The name was originally inspired by a Danish phrase, *leg godt*, or "play well," and was chosen in part because the company's eight employees agreed that it was catchy and easy to remember.[10]

A new name was proof that the toymaker wasn't just biding his time until the economy could once again support the more important work of carpentry. On the contrary, Christiansen would often insist that his new venture was every bit as important as that of a practical carpenter.

LEGO's meaning also reflected the real heart behind Christiansen's pivot from carpentry to toymaking. At his core, Christiansen was a joyful, childlike man who loved making quality playthings for children. That passion for play became a driving force behind his work.

While toymaking may have started out as a passion project, it soon proved to be a profitable one as well. By the end of 1935, the newly renamed toy factory had made 17,200 kroner in profits (equivalent to around 64,000 US dollars today), double those of the previous year. By the end of 1936, that number doubled yet again.

After years of setbacks, debt, and grief, things were finally looking up for Christiansen. He had a new bride, a new name for his company, and a new vision from God that gave him confidence for the future.

The following years were filled with one blessing after another. Sofie gave birth to a healthy baby girl named Ulla in 1935. By 1940, his son Godtfred—no longer the little boy who once burned down the workshop—was made a foreman at LEGO and was already proving to be a capable business partner. That year, profits reached yet another record high.

Two years later, in 1942, the third fire swept through the workshop. Despite the initial shock of the loss, Christiansen was miraculously able to sell enough salvaged inventory to not only fund a rebuild but also pay off all remaining debts to friends and family. By the end of the year, a new workshop was ready for production, and the company had grown to about forty employees.

In the nearly thirty years since he arrived in Billund, Christiansen had seen God carry him and his company through a dramatic series of ups and downs. Each one served to deepen his faith a bit more. By 1943, Christiansen was going to need that faith more than ever, because with World War II in full swing, the Nazis were making their way to LEGO's front door.

CHAPTER 27

W*ham!* The door to the LEGO offices slammed open, causing everyone to jump in surprise. Ole Kirk Christiansen's son and business partner Godtfred stood and faced the front, steeling himself for what might come next.

The Nazi officer closed the distance between them in a few short strides. Then, raising his arm to gesture around the room, he quickly fired off a series of commands in German.

It was obvious he wanted to take control of the expansive workshop for his soldiers' use, but Godtfred used the language barrier to his advantage, fixing the intruder with a cold, blank stare.

After a few tense moments, the officer spun on his heels and marched out of the room, slamming the door behind him once more. Everyone in the office let out a shaky breath, exchanging nervous glances with one another but hardly daring to move.

To everyone's surprise, the officer didn't return to exert his will—not that day, not ever. Miraculously, God preserved the LEGO workshop from occupation.

The Christiansen home was another matter.

The two German officers who showed up there demanding a place to live were not so easily put off by feigned confusion. And Christiansen didn't need to speak their language to understand they were moving into the first floor of his home immediately.

Over the following months, the family would live "as sheep in the midst of wolves" in their own home (Matthew 10:16, ESV). Anytime Christiansen crossed paths with the soldiers downstairs or around town, he kept the interactions as brief as possible. To their faces, he was polite and respectful. They had no idea what he was up to behind their backs.

Not even Godtfred knew that the toy shipments leaving the factory in horse-drawn buggies weren't always as they seemed. Christiansen had secretly become a volunteer leader in Denmark's underground resistance army and was leveraging his business to smuggle hand grenades and other weapons in empty toy boxes.

More publicly, he also served as the head of the town watchmen, a local group that stepped into the gap to maintain order when German forces disbanded the Danish police.

Remarkably, his hands-on work as a leader in the community and the underground resistance seemed only to strengthen Christiansen's resolve that his work as a toymaker mattered too.

He did everything he could to keep production running amid rationing, blackouts, and occupation. In the summer months, he worked alongside employees out in the marsh, gathering materials they could burn in the winter to heat the factory. And when blackouts cut their workdays short, he adjusted the team's schedule to make the most of daylight hours.

Christiansen sensed that even in wartime, toymaking was a worthy pursuit because high-quality toys could deliver joy and hope to Danish families who needed a reminder that there was still light in the world.

LEGO's sales numbers proved that Christiansen's instincts were right. Throughout World War II, the company continued to break records, reaching 375,000 kroner in sales in 1945 and totaling over one million kroner across the five years of German occupation (equivalent to around 835,000 and 2.2 million US dollars today).

If anything, the war was financially good for LEGO, but its owner still worked and prayed for it to end. "Humanity's interests come first, material interests second," Christiansen told his bookkeeper.[11]

Privately, he journaled, "The war may be why we have had such a large [profit], yet that does not mean we wish the war to continue. We wish for peace across the whole world, and pray, 'Lord, take this into your hands!'"[12]

On May 8, 1945, the prayers of Ole Kirk Christiansen and millions of others were answered when Germany surrendered, marking the end of World War II in Europe.

Many small towns experienced horrifying displays of mob justice in the days that followed liberation. Without a police force to preserve order, vigilantes committed brutal acts of violence against German refugees and even neighbors they perceived to be traitors. But not so in Billund—thanks in large part to the town's toymaker.

Each night, Christiansen, his bookkeeper, and the chairman of the town council armed themselves and patrolled the streets. Instead of hunting down collaborators, they stood up for justice by protecting German refugees asleep in the town hall and ensuring any Nazi sympathizers would have their chance at a fair trial.

As he paced back and forth in the quiet of the night, Christiansen had time to reflect on all the ways God had protected his family and blessed his business throughout the war. Across Denmark, LEGO was becoming a household name. The company's wooden cars, trains, and blocks were reaching peak popularity.

But Christiansen had no way of knowing the war's impact on the toy industry was just beginning. After a few years of rapid developments in wartime production, a new material was poised to take the consumer world by storm: plastic. It would soon change the toy industry—and the future of LEGO—forever.

CHAPTER 28

We never should have got that bloody plastics machine, Dad. It's bankrupting us!" shouted Godtfred.[13]

Ole Kirk Christiansen, sitting behind his desk, studied his four adult sons. Twenty-six-year-old Godtfred had been arguing with him for months over the decision to experiment with plastic production, but this time he'd brought all his brothers for backup.

Godtfred had plenty of reasons to be angry. For one thing, the machine in question, which had arrived at LEGO a few months before in November of 1947, was currently housed in his basement. His home was filled with the smell of melted plastic, and the incessant banging was constantly waking up his newborn son, Kjeld. The machine was driving him and his wife crazy.

On top of that, when the family patriarch was down there running the plastics machine at all hours, he wasn't much help in running the company. After a lifetime of hearing his father extol the virtues of masterfully made wooden toys, Godtfred couldn't believe how distracted the man had become by this newfangled nonsense.

And then, as in any family business, there was the biggest sticking point of all: money. Godtfred wasn't exaggerating when he said that plastics were bankrupting LEGO. Christiansen was spending money faster than the company could make it.

But it didn't really matter how many reasons Godtfred gave for pulling the plug on plastics. Christiansen saw just as many reasons to keep going.

Plastics, he was convinced, were the future. Already, items made of plastic were appearing on store shelves around the world. And he'd heard that other toy companies were running their own experiments in plastic production.

Whichever companies got it right would be able to produce more toys in less time and with fewer people.

And this didn't mean giving up on quality craftsmanship either. On the contrary, plastic production would allow LEGO to sell more durable and hygienic toys that would appeal to parents as much as their children.

But perhaps the strongest reason of all was the one Christiansen had been literally carrying around in his pocket since the summer: small plastic bricks.

The colorful bricks were invented in England by Hilary Page, founder of Kiddicraft. But in a decision that would shape the toy industry forever, Page took out a patent only in England, France, and Switzerland. Denmark wasn't on the list.

When Christiansen first received a sample of the bricks from a plastics machine salesman, he was immediately mesmerized. He'd always thought that the best toys were the ones children wanted to play with long after unwrapping them at Christmas. These bricks, he believed, were exactly that. There was no way he was going to give up on the plastics machine until he took these bricks to the Danish market.

No one knows exactly how the heated confrontation between father and sons concluded that day, but we do know who won the argument. After another year of Christiansen's noisy experiments and a few tweaks to the Kiddicraft design, LEGO introduced its "Automatic Binding Bricks" to the world in 1949.

They were, as it turned out, met with the same reaction as Page's version in England: lackluster sales and disinterested shop owners. Kiddicraft moved on to other toys. As far as Godtfred was concerned, it was time for LEGO to do the same. He'd tried to remain patient, but the idea was clearly a bust. Once more, he gathered his three brothers for support and led the charge back into his dad's office.

Christiansen sat in silence as his sons ran through the litany of reasons he should give up. When it was his turn to speak, his rebuttal was simple: "Don't you have enough faith, boys? I have prayed to God, and I believe in these bricks! We have to leave this in God's hands, and everything will work out."[14]

His sons would later recall, "We just slunk quietly out of the office, and that was the end of the discussion."[15]

Despite their disagreements, Christiansen gave Godtfred even more responsibility on his thirtieth birthday, in the summer of 1951. Then, in 1952, Christiansen decided to expand the LEGO factories yet again. The project cost 350,000 kroner (around 582,000 US dollars today)—a sum, Godtfred reminded him, they simply could not afford.

As usual, Christiansen wasn't basing his decisions on the company's ledgers. He was basing them on faith. With that miraculous vision of a bustling factory still crystal clear in his mind, he forged ahead with his plans.

Godtfred was apoplectic. He resigned from LEGO, gathered his family, and left the country. With tears in his eyes, Christiansen watched him go. But just one week later, Godtfred returned home.

LEGO was in his blood. He couldn't bear to leave, but he also had a sinking suspicion the company wouldn't survive much longer. "We're relying on your faith now, not mine," he told his father with a sigh.

But Godtfred wouldn't have to run on borrowed faith for long. The big break for LEGO's bricks was just around the corner.

CHAPTER 29

Ole Kirk Christiansen knew he was running out of time. The first sign was a stroke that put him in the hospital in 1951, not long after he promoted Godtfred to junior managing director. He recovered without major complications, much to everyone's relief, but he could sense that his strength was dwindling. It was time, he knew, for Godtfred to start taking the reins of LEGO.

Godtfred was ready. For decades, he'd watched his father "pray and work," and he was committed to doing the same. The first task at hand was to find a way to fund the factory expansion to which his father had already committed. The solution, he decided, was to take LEGO into new markets, beyond the borders of Denmark.

As Godtfred traveled to surrounding countries in the early 1950s, a conviction began to form within him: If LEGO was to succeed on the international stage, the company needed to focus. LEGO was producing 256 different toys, made of both wood and plastic, and they couldn't scale up with all of them at once. Godtfred needed one idea, one toy that would be easy to mass produce and stand the test of time.

He only needed to walk downstairs to his basement to find his answer. The space that once held the plastics machine was now his children's playroom. And with access to all of LEGO's inventory, there was just one toy that kept them occupied for hours on end—their grandfather's favorite plastic bricks.

Despite a recent rebrand as "LEGO Bricks," the toy still hadn't taken off. But watching his children build towers large enough to hide in, Godtfred began to admit that his dad was right. This was a toy that inspired unparalleled play and imagination.

Better yet, he realized, the more LEGO Bricks a child had, the more that child would want. The company could roll out a full "LEGO System in Play" with individual sets that worked separately or together. The potential for sales was nearly limitless.

Godtfred could finally see a future for his father's plastic bricks—and that's when LEGO really began to take off. In the second half of the 1950s, the company's annual profits climbed from two million to ten million kroner (equivalent to a jump from 2.7 million to 13.8 million US dollars today), while the number of staff jumped dramatically from 140 to 450 employees.

Under Godtfred's leadership, his father's vision for LEGO was becoming a reality. Only one problem continued to needle him: The hollow bricks didn't always stick together as well as he would like.

The minor flaw didn't seem to be hindering sales at all, and most business leaders would have likely waved off such a small imperfection in the face of rapid growth. But then, most business leaders weren't raised by Ole Kirk Christiansen. For Godtfred, the issue likely brought to mind one of the most formative experiences of his life.

As a young boy in the 1930s, Godtfred was already showing signs of a natural business acumen. He was working in his dad's new toy business when he saw an opportunity to improve efficiency. They could ship out an order of wooden ducks much faster if they gave each toy two coats of varnish instead of three, saving the company both time and money.

He sent out an order of the two-coat ducks and then proudly reported his success to his father. To Godtfred's surprise and embarrassment, Christiansen demanded his son go out and fetch the entire order to give them the third coat of varnish.

Godtfred had deemed the order to be good enough, but Christiansen wanted his sons and employees to understand that "only the best is good enough."[16] Cutting corners to prioritize efficiency over quality was unacceptable. Businesses, Christiansen believed, had a responsibility to care for customers, which meant committing to quality in every detail.

By 1957, Christiansen no longer had the strength or desire to oversee his son's work, but he was about to see a biblical principle in action: "Train up a child in the way he should go, and when he is old he will not depart from it" (Proverbs 22:6, NKJV).

When the first customer complaints about LEGO creations falling apart reached Godtfred, he immediately stopped everything to sit down with the company's leaders and find a solution. After a few days of focused experiments, they had it: a system of tubes and studs that allowed the bricks to "click" together and stay together until intentionally pulled apart.

Godtfred rushed to Copenhagen to patent not only the winning idea but also every idea they'd tried along the way. He knew this design would be the very thing to set them apart from the competitors popping up to capitalize on LEGO's success.

On January 28, 1958, Godtfred walked out the doors of the patent office with a piece of paper that placed LEGO firmly on its trajectory toward becoming a global powerhouse in the toy industry. But Godtfred was going to have to navigate that path without the help of his father.

Just six weeks after the patent was awarded, the company's remarkable founder would be gone.

CHAPTER 30

On March 15, 1958, the street in front of Ole Kirk Christiansen's home was quiet, even though nearly every one of Billund's residents was gathered there. The people who had once rushed to the family's aid in fire and loss were now coming around to say goodbye.

Everyone could remember the sound of Christiansen's booming laugh as he played in the streets with the town's children. But now the only sounds were those of muffled sniffles and the crunch of spruce twigs underfoot as Christiansen's pallbearers placed his coffin in the back of a hearse.

When the hearse pulled away from the home and began its slow ride toward Grene Parish Church, Christiansen's wife, children, and grandchildren followed on foot. Friends and neighbors filled the street behind them in a show of support, and flags flew at half-staff as the entire town grieved the loss of LEGO's founder.

Every corner of the little parish church was soon filled, and extra pews spilled out onto the porch. The priest reminded everyone present that for the Christian, death does not have the final word. He also commended his friend on a life well lived, saying, "[Christiansen] remained faithful to the vision he had in his youth, and there can be no doubt that this shaped all of his very capable efforts, life, and work."[17]

Nearly every person listening could have told a unique story of how Christiansen's life and faithfulness had affected them personally.

Some shared how their families had flourished thanks to the meaningful work they found at LEGO. Others recounted memories from the church services the founder led for employees every weekday. Still others remembered all the way back to the company's early days, when a young Ole Kirk Christiansen gathered around the table with his family and a handful of employees for devotions and meals.

But even those who had never heard Christiansen pray, sing a hymn, or share the gospel had been blessed by the fruits of his faith and work.

There were those whose families were spared worse fates in the Great Depression because the carpenter on the edge of town had forgiven their debts. There were those who had survived the tumultuous days following World War II only because Christiansen stood in the gap for them. And of course, there were many families who were closer to one another because a jovial toymaker had taught them how to *leg godt* or "play well" together.

The decades to follow would reveal that Ole Kirk Christiansen's impact would outlive not only him but also everyone gathered for his funeral that day.

Because of his legacy of excellence, LEGO bricks were declared in 2004 to be the most popular toy of the previous century. Because of his legacy of loving his family well, his great-grandson assumed the role of CEO in 2017, representing the fourth generation to lead the company. And because of his legacy of delighting in play, his hometown of Billund is now upheld as a role model worldwide for how child-centered design and creative imagination can change a city—and the world—for the better.

Ole Kirk Christiansen didn't live to see everything LEGO would become, but he did live long enough to hear his son affirm the value of his life and work.

Just a few months before his death, Christiansen attended a New Year's party to mark the end of the company's twenty-fifth year in the toy business. In the middle of a speech to employees, his son Godtfred turned to lock eyes with his father as he said, "You have created something of genuine social benefit, Dad!…All of us gathered here will continue to strive to do our best…our motto [like yours] remains 'Pray and work.'"[18]

Pray and work. That simple motto guided Ole Kirk Christiansen through a complicated life filled with loss, grief, and trials but also laughter, love, and success. At the end of it all, he could look back and say, like Apostle Paul, "I have fought the good fight, I have finished the race, I have kept the faith" (2 Timothy 4:7).

Christiansen had done what every mere Christian longs to do. In the face of great adversity, he worked with excellence, loved God, and loved people.

Nearly a hundred years later, his life still beckons all who know his incredible story to do the same.

THREE WAYS TO GLORIFY GOD IN YOUR WORK
AS SEEN IN THE LIFE OF OLE KIRK CHRISTIANSEN

I (Jordan) picked up a copy of the book *The LEGO Story* purely out of fascination with LEGO as a business. But as soon as I started to read the story of LEGO's founder, I was entranced. I felt I had struck gold. It wasn't just the drama of Christiansen's life that knocked me out. It was his *faithfulness*. Ever since, I've carried Christiansen around in my mind as a three-dimensional model of how to worship God as a modern mere Christian. I hope you will do the same because through his life we see at least three ways to glorify God in our work today.

I. MERE CHRISTIANS GLORIFY GOD BY PERSEVERING THROUGH TRIALS IN FAITH.

Ole Kirk Christiansen suffered more than most of us ever will. He watched his life's work literally go up in flames not once, not twice, but *three* times. He spent years teetering on the brink of bankruptcy. And in the span of just a few days, he suffered the unimaginable loss of his wife *and* a child.

And yet, Christiansen consistently joined God's servant Job in saying, "The LORD gave, and the LORD hath taken away; blessed be the name of the LORD" (Job 1:21, KJV). He clung tightly to the promise of Romans 8:28 that "in *all* things"—even the most terrible ones—"God works for the good of those who love him."

By God's grace, Christiansen was able to see some of that "good" on this side of eternity. He saw how God used economic hardships to pivot him away from a traditional carpentry business to making toys. He saw how God used the tragic loss of one wife to lead to another who would fund the founding of LEGO.

But there's no doubt that Christiansen went to the grave without comprehending how God would use other tragedies for good. After all, what human can understand the good of losing a child? And yet, Christiansen had faith that somehow God was *doing* good to him even when it didn't *feel* good to him.

Christiansen glorified God by persevering through unimaginable trials in faith—often by journaling his prayers. You and I can do the same today. As a practical response to Christiansen's story, let me encourage you to pull out a pen and some paper or a note on your phone and journal three things.

First, *journal a lament to God about your current trials*. Yes, you are to "consider it pure joy…whenever you face trials of many kinds, because you know that the testing of your faith produces perseverance" (James 1:2-3). But God *also* invites us to lament about the thorns and thistles that fight against us (see Psalm 34:17). You better believe Ole Kirk Christiansen lamented the loss of his factories and family. God will welcome your prayer of lament as well.

Second, *journal about how God has used past trials for good*. Hindsight is twenty-twenty. It is *much* easier to see how God has used past trials for good than it is to see how he might use your current trials for good. So think back to a painful moment in your career—the time you lost your job, the time your bank account was nearing zero, or the time you faced genuine persecution for your faith—and journal about how you've seen God use that trial for his glory and your good.

Finally, after reflecting on God's faithfulness in the past, *journal in faith that God will keep his promise to use your current trials for good*. You may find it helpful to write out these verses as you pray: James 1:2, Romans 5:3, Romans 8:28, 2 Samuel 16:12.

2. MERE CHRISTIANS GLORIFY GOD BY EMBRACING PLAY AND "USELESS" WORK.

All throughout Scripture, we see God doing work that most people in our utilitarian-obsessed culture would describe as pointless and impractical.

In Genesis 2:9, it says that God made trees that were useful for food *and* beautiful. In Job 38:25-26, God said that he sends "torrents of rain…to water a land where no one lives," apparently just for the fun of it. And in Revelation, we're told that God has covered his eternal city, the New Jerusalem, with 5,600 *miles* of emeralds, rubies, and "every kind of precious stone" (Revelation 21:15-21).

What purpose do beautiful trees, desert rain, and 5,600 miles of jewels serve? My guess is none—*and that is precisely the point!* Because as theologian Gustavo Gutiérrez says, "Utility is not the primary reason for God's action."[19] Sometimes God does things for the pure joy and play of it. So, we as his image-bearers can too.

I don't think anyone understood this better than Ole Kirk Christiansen. When he decided to pivot away from his traditional carpentry business to building a toy factory, almost everyone told Christiansen he was crazy. The world was in crisis—in the pit of the Great Depression! People needed food and shelter, Christiansen's friends told him, not yo-yos and toy cars.

But Christiansen disagreed. In his own playful life and the life of the business he created to help others "play well," Christiansen demonstrated a deep understanding that mere Christians can glorify God by embracing fun, beauty, play, and "useless" work because their heavenly Father does the same.

You don't have to be alleviating poverty, prosecuting human traffickers, or curing diseases to honor God through your vocation (as good and important as that work is). You can please him by designing beautiful charcuterie boards, planning joyous events, and building the next great toy company. So, if you do work the world tends to view as trivial and useless, *lean into it* today with all your heart, knowing that the Lord "delights in every detail" of the lives of the godly (see Psalm 37:23, NLT).

3. MERE CHRISTIANS GLORIFY GOD BY COMMITTING THEMSELVES TO THE MINISTRY OF EXCELLENCE.

From requiring that each of LEGO's early wooden ducks received three coats of paint to fighting for the perfect interlocking LEGO brick, Ole Kirk Christiansen consistently demonstrated a deep commitment to excellence in his craft.

But don't miss the *why* behind that commitment. Christiansen was never recorded as saying anything like, "Only the best is good enough *because that's how we maximize profits.*" Only the best was good enough because Christiansen understood that mere Christians glorify God through the ministry of excellence.

In 1 Corinthians 10:31, the apostle Paul commands that in "whatever you do, do it all for the glory of God," which means to act in ways that reflect God's character to others. And what is one of God's primary characteristics as a worker? Excellence!

Commenting on the carpenter whom Christiansen called Savior, the novelist Dorothy L. Sayers said, "No crooked table legs or ill-fitting drawers ever, I dare swear, came out of the carpenter's shop at Nazareth…work must be good work before it can call itself God's work…The only Christian work is good work well done."[20]

PART IV

HANNAH MORE

POET AND EDUCATOR

HOW TO GLORIFY GOD BY INSULATING WITHOUT ISOLATING, REDEEMING POP CULTURE, AND EXUDING HOLY AUDACITY

CHAPTER 31

Hannah More wasn't present the night her career as a playwright died a public and embarrassing death, but she knew it soon enough. The story was in all the papers.

More's first play, *Percy*, had been a massive success in 1777—earning an unheard of twenty-two-night run in which each performance elicited thunderous applause. Feeling the pressure to replicate that success, More agonized under the weight of sky-high expectations every day she worked on her second play, *The Fatal Falsehood*.

After giving approval for her play to be produced in London's Covent Garden, an anxious More couldn't even bring herself to appear for the performance. Her sister Sally attended instead and then mailed a letter with her report: The play "was indeed greatly received…When the curtain dropped, the house absolutely shouted."[1]

But then, on the second night, the applause was cut short by shrieking from the balcony: "That's mine! That's mine!" All eyes turned to the balcony where Hannah Cowley, a rival playwright, thrust an accusatory finger at the stage and then promptly fainted.[2]

Journalists and theater critics wasted no time in rushing to print Cowley's claims that More had plagiarized her work. Hannah More, shocked by the allegations being volleyed at her, published a statement: "I am under the necessity of solemnly declaring, that I never saw, heard, or read, a single line of Mrs. Cowley's [yet-unpublished] tragedy."[3]

In the end, there was no evidence that the plagiarism charges were justified, but that didn't stop Cowley from taking a parting shot: "by some WONDERFUL coincidence, Miss More and I have but one common stock of ideas between us."[4]

Ironically, the falsehood levied by Cowley proved fatal for *The Fatal False-hood* and for More's career as a playwright. The play's run ended abruptly after just four nights, and More never wrote or attended another play again.

Having her name dragged through the mud only solidified feelings More had been quietly developing for a while—that the world of theater and fame, with its "vanity that tempted and repelled her simultaneously" could not satisfy.[5]

After her rise and fall as London's "much-sought-after darling," More felt a pull to retreat from London's snobby social circles so that she might better focus on her relationship with and service to God.[6]

And she likely would have done exactly that if not for the intervention of her friend William Wilberforce, the famous abolitionist and member of Parliament.

It was Wilberforce who convinced More to stay in the cultural center of her time to work alongside him for the freedom of slaves. But More didn't do that work as a missionary or a pastor's wife. In fact, despite ardent proposals from two different men she loved and a six-year engagement to one of them, she never married at all.

Instead, she worked as an author who outsold her contemporary Jane Austen ten to one. She worked as a poet who had kings and queens requesting handwritten copies of her work. And she worked as an educator who laid the foundation of what would become the public school system in Great Britain.

That is to say, More worked as a mere Christian leveraging the written word and education for the glory of God and the good of others. As a result, she became "nothing less than the most influential woman of her time."[7]

For years, Christian missionaries regularly named orphaned African girls in their care "Hannah More" to honor More's unmatched contributions to abolishing the slave trade. And while those young girls never forgot her name, history largely has. Instead, Wilberforce's work as a politician has garnered most of the credit for abolition in Great Britain.

But Wilberforce himself confessed that he became "conscious of the false-hood" of his once-held belief that "individuals who are not in parliament seldom have an opportunity of doing good to considerable numbers." What changed his mind? "Witness Mrs. Hannah More," he argued, "and all those who labour with the pen."[8]

Historians agree: "How Wilberforce came to be the chief champion of abolition—and how he was able to succeed in ending the slave trade in Great Britain in 1807, after twenty years of battling—has everything to do with Hannah More."[9]

In the following pages, you'll discover the dramatic yet little-known story of how a poet helped end the slave trade. It is a story filled with romance and heartbreak, celebrity and humility, and belonging and loss. It is also full of immense wisdom for the mere Christians of today.

Hannah More's life serves as a reminder that Christians can glorify God through culture and not just the pulpit or politics. She is proof that Christians are most impactful when they insulate yet refuse to isolate from the world. And ultimately, her surprising boldness will inspire you to be audacious in your own work, knowing God is with you wherever you go.

CHAPTER 32

"C ome! Let us ride to London to see bishops and booksellers!"[10]

The precocious little girl beckoning one and all to join her on the journey of a lifetime was perched atop a train going nowhere, because it wasn't a train at all. It was a row of wooden chairs lined up in a schoolhouse just outside of Bristol, England, where all the students had gone home for the day.

But Hannah More wasn't a student, and this wasn't her school. It was her home. She, her four sisters, and her parents lived in the two-story stone schoolhouse where she'd been born on February 2, 1745. Her poor but devoted father, Jacob More, served as a schoolteacher for the sons of local families.

The More family couldn't afford a trip to London—or anywhere else, for that matter—but that didn't stop Hannah from going there in her imagination. She longed to see the bustling excitement of the city whose "bishops and booksellers" were changing the world with their words.

From the time Hannah taught herself to read at three or four years old, she'd sensed a power in words that drew her in. When she discovered Shakespeare for the first time, she was so captivated by his writing she could hardly sleep that night.

Already an aspiring writer, young Hannah only ever wanted one gift for birthdays and Christmas: fresh, crisp paper she could fill to the margins with her own essays and poems. Only two lines survive from her very first poem, which she penned at the age of four:

> This road leads to a great city,
> Which is more populous than witty.

The satirical take on her hometown of Bristol was an early sign of intelligence beyond her years, a sign that filled her father with a complex mixture of pride and concern. Because in the 1700s, a woman's education was meant to prepare her for one thing and one thing only.

Jean-Jacques Rousseau reflected the prevailing opinions of the time when he wrote that "the whole education of women ought to relate to men. To please men, to be useful to them...to make their lives agreeable and sweet—these are the duties of women at all times, and they ought to be taught them from childhood."[11]

Nearly everyone agreed that a real and rigorous education belonged to men exclusively, since experts argued that "intense thought spoils a lady's features" or could even "cause significant harm to [women's] reproductive organs and their nervous systems."[12]

And yet, an educator like Jacob More couldn't help but be enthralled by his fourth daughter's remarkable intellect, watching with awe as Hannah engaged even educated doctors in lively discussions of literature.

Striking a compromise, Jacob More carefully selected what he viewed as appropriate subjects for his five daughters—shepherding them toward language and literature and away from math and science. Ultimately, he would shape his girls' education not around pleasing men but toward careers as teachers, the one profession he knew would be deemed acceptable by the prevailing culture.

But Hannah would be influenced by what was going on outside the walls of the schoolhouse as much as she was by the lessons she heard within them. Despite Hannah's cheeky verse claiming that her small town wasn't "witty," Bristol was becoming the center of a nationwide revival.

John Wesley opened his first Methodist chapel just a few miles down the road from the More family home, urging Christians to move beyond "the understanding" of "right opinions" and to adopt a "religion of the heart"—a genuine, holistic faith that moved beyond intellectual assent.[13] His sermons stirred new excitement in the Church of England, of which the Mores were faithful members.

While it's unknown if Hannah ever met Wesley, she was certainly not immune to the religious fervor sweeping through her town. When she wasn't climbing atop make-believe trains, she was standing on play pulpits instead, delivering passionate sermons for her family.

By the time Hannah was thirteen years old, her attention turned from imaginary itineraries and pretend preaching to the very real work of her older sisters who placed an ad in the *Bristol Journal*: "On Monday after Easter will be opened a School for Young Ladies by Mary More and Sisters, where will be carefully taught French, Reading, Writing, Arithmetic, and Needlework...A Dancing Master will properly attend."[14]

The More sisters were ready to embark on the path laid out for them by their father. Hannah enrolled as a student in her sisters' school, and by the age of sixteen, she, too, was teaching classes.

The family venture was an immediate success. Even after the school outgrew its original accommodations and opened a new location, it maintained a lengthy waiting list of affluent families hoping to enroll their daughters. Over the next thirty years, the school would prove to be a source of stability and security for the More sisters until they retired.

But God didn't intend for Hannah to retire as a teacher like her sisters. A very real trip to London was in her future—and with it, a new career as the fastest-rising star in British pop culture.

CHAPTER 33

The first time Hannah More entered Bristol's newly built theater, she didn't waltz through the front door because, technically speaking, it didn't have one. As far as the government was concerned, the theater didn't exist at all.

After failing to obtain the royal patent required for producing plays, the theater group's very existence was illegal. So, in an effort to stay under the radar, they called themselves "The Circle" and falsely advertised their opening night in 1766 as a musical concert. Then they recruited the assistance of Mr. Foote next door.

Through whispered instructions passed among elite social circles, Bristol's residents learned to knock on Mr. Foote's door, sneak through his home and backyard, and slip quietly into the secret entrance of the 1,600-seat theater if they wanted to catch a play.

When acclaimed London actor William Powell moved to Bristol to manage the new theater—and promptly enrolled his daughter in More's class—More saw an opportunity. After introducing herself to Powell, she became a regular at Mr. Foote's front door, often attending performances with students in tow.

Before long, More casually raised a topic she'd been dying to discuss with Powell ever since his daughter landed in her class: Did he know that she had, in fact, written a play of her own?

Indeed, just three years prior, an eighteen-year-old More had written *The Search after Happiness* for her students to perform after failing to find a play she deemed both engaging and appropriate enough for an all-female cast of teenage girls.

The play itself betrayed the real reason More was so eager to build a friendship with Powell. In it, one character voices a lament about the public perception of female writers: "Tho' should we still the rhyming trade pursue, The men will shun us,—and the women, too."[15]

More instinctively understood that success as a writer always depends more on who you know than what you know. And for an aspiring female playwright in 1766, a connection to an established theater professional like Powell was essential to having her work read and performed outside the walls of her family's school.

Powell proved receptive to More's networking and, more importantly, her work itself. When the theater produced *Hamlet* in its first season, Powell opened the performance by delivering a prologue More had written. Sitting in the audience that evening, More watched in awe as a real, famous actor delivered words she'd written—and on the very stage where one of Shakespeare's most famous works was about to be performed.

The rush she felt inspired her to continue advocating for her work any chance she got. When the famous actor and orator Thomas Sheridan came to Bristol to deliver a series of lectures, More rushed home from the performance to pen a poem lauding his talents ("The well-earn'd praise, O Sheridan, were thine!").[16] A mutual friend delivered the poem, and the flattered Sheridan immediately asked to meet its author.

Although More's audacious networking skills benefited her career, the relationships she formed along the way were genuine. Sheridan remained a close friend and ardent supporter of her work throughout their lives, and the entire Powell family welcomed More into their fold.

In the classroom, More continued to hone her skills as a storyteller, leveraging drama and imagination as tools for instilling good Christian morals in her students. When she taught Bible and literature, she wanted her students to feel immersed in the stories, to "see Christ walking on the water...[of the River] Thames."[17]

Her storytelling talents were a refreshing departure from the rote repetition and dry lectures more commonly employed by other teachers. Despite her gifts as an educator, it would soon become clear that God was using her years in the classroom as a training ground for a bigger stage.

The play she'd written for her students was going to be her ticket to London—and fame. But her friend William Powell wouldn't live to see it.

Just three years into his role as Bristol's theater manager, the ever-dramatic

Powell flung himself into some wet grass after overheating in a game of tennis. To everyone's shock, the larger-than-life actor fell seriously ill as a result.

More came to the Powell home to visit and even offered to sit by William's bedside so his wife could rest. But while his wife was away, William took a sudden turn for the worse. In a dramatic but heartbreaking end fit for the stage, he took his final breath in More's arms.

In the end, William Powell was a dear friend gone too soon, not the man who would take More's career to the next level. Another William would pave the way for that—but first, he was going to break her heart.

CHAPTER 34

Hannah More had heard rumors about the sprawling Belmont estate a few miles outside of Bristol, but nothing could have prepared her for seeing it herself—or for meeting the man who called it home.

More first visited William Turner's estate as a guest of his cousin. With its stables full of horses, carriages at the ready, carefully maintained gardens, and sweeping panoramic views, Belmont was the perfect place to spend a holiday.

And then there was Turner himself.

The forty-two-year-old bachelor "was a man of strict honour and integrity, had received a liberal education, and, among other recommendations of an intellectual character, had cultivated a taste for poetry."[18]

So when a beautiful young poet showed up at his estate, "the consequence was natural. She was very clever and fascinating, and he was generous and sensible; he became attached."[19]

The romance that ensued was a dream come true for a poor teacher's daughter. In Turner, More saw an opportunity to marry rich and match wits with a man who wasn't threatened by her talents as a writer—a truth he proved with grand gestures throughout their courtship.

On one visit to Belmont, More was delighted to learn Turner had engraved lines of her poetry on wooden plaques and posted them throughout his gardens. On another, she found he had prepared a place for her to write—a quiet cottage where she wouldn't be interrupted.

When Turner proposed marriage, More accepted and immediately began preparing for a new life running Belmont at his side: quitting her job, investing in the wardrobe expected of a woman in her position, and consulting with her fiancé on matters of his estate and gardens.

But as the wedding date drew near, Turner approached More about postponing their nuptials. She agreed, and they set a new date. As the new date grew near, an anxious Turner once again asked to postpone, and a disappointed More once again agreed.

The engagement stretched on for nearly six years before the bells at Clifton Parish Church in Bristol announced that their wedding day had come at last. More, surrounded by her sisters and friends, peered out the window, anticipating the arrival of her groom.

She was still looking for his familiar form among the crowds when she heard a soft knock at the door. It was the groom's best friend and best man. The embarrassment on his face said far more than Turner's letter of apology in his hands. He wasn't coming. The wedding was off.

Remarkably, once the guests had been notified and sent home, Turner had yet another change of heart and begged More for one more chance to meet her at the altar, but "her sisters and friends interfered, and would not permit her to be so treated and trifled with." Bolstered by their indignation on her behalf, More "persevered in keeping up her determination not to renew the engagement."[20]

Her fairytale had been merely a facade, and a devastated More left town in search of some fresh air and privacy. In Weston-super-Mare at a seaside resort, fresh air would be easy enough to come by, but when she met Dr. James Langhorne upon arrival, she quickly forgot her desire for privacy altogether.

Dr. Langhorne didn't share Turner's inexplicable fear of commitment. He'd been married—and widowed—twice. As an established poet and clergyman, the tragic, handsome figure had a way with both women and words. And in the beautiful, brokenhearted Hannah More, he found a willing recipient of his affections.

A vacation romance began. The pair left little notes for one another to find around the resort and frequently slipped away from the other guests for leisurely horseback rides along the beach. On one of those rides, Dr. Langhorne paused to write a poem for More in the sand:

Along the shore
Walk'd Hannah More;
Waves! let this record last:

Sooner shall ye,

Proud earth and sea,

Than what she writes, be past.

With a smile, More grabbed a stick and drew her response on the shore:

Some firmer basis, polish'd Langhorne, choose,

To write the dictates of thy charming muse;

Thy strains in solid characters rehearse,

And be thy tablet lasting as thy verse.[21]

As the first signs of fall appeared, Langhorne expressed his desires for more than a summer fling. But her recent humiliation was all too fresh, and More was resolved to avoid "a similar entanglement."[22] Not even Langhorne's proposal of marriage changed her mind.

Upon her return to Bristol, yet another proposal awaited her: William Turner pleaded again for one more chance to make More his wife. Still, she refused. But her sisters and friends weren't quite ready to let Turner off the hook for stringing More along and wasting her prime marrying years.

Family friend Dr. James Stonhouse paid Turner a visit. Without More's knowledge, he argued that Turner should provide an annuity to the woman who had put her life on hold for six years and spent a great deal of money in preparation for a marriage that never materialized.

Turner happily agreed to an annuity of two hundred pounds a year (the equivalent of 57,860 US dollars today), which More reluctantly accepted at the insistence of Stonhouse and her sisters. The sum couldn't heal her broken heart, but it could cover her living expenses and grant her the exceedingly rare opportunity to pursue a writing career without the support of a husband.

Once they knew her future was secure, More's loving sisters weren't above teasing her a bit. Younger sister Patty joked to a friend, "This Poet of ours is taken care of and may sit down on her large behind and read, no, devour, as many books as she pleases without molestation."[23]

With her financial needs met by Turner's annuity, More would never enter another romantic relationship. Remarkably, all four of her sisters remained single as well, forming a tight-knit circle into which no other man ever successfully gained entry.

As for Turner, he never got over the one who got away. For the rest of his life, whether alone or with friends, he always raised his first glass of wine in a toast to Hannah More.

Until the day he died, More's "virtues and excellences were his favorite theme among his intimate friends," and he reassured himself that "Providence had overruled his wish to be her husband in order to preserve her for higher things."[24]

But as a newly wealthy twenty-eight-year-old woman, More wasn't giving much thought to "higher things." It was the high life of high society that she couldn't wait to experience in London.

CHAPTER 35

By the time Hannah More embarked on her first trip to London in 1774, her childhood dream of seeing bishops and booksellers had been replaced by a longing to meet publishers and performers. The trip took two days by stage-coach, giving her plenty of time to think over her itinerary.

Her first priority was to meet her new publisher. After advocating for the annuity from William Turner, Stonhouse had proved a continued source of support for More. It was thanks to his help and connections that *The Search after Happiness* had finally gone to print ten years after she wrote it in her sisters' schoolhouse.

Aside from her meeting with the publisher, More would be free to explore London. Most of all, she hoped to cross paths with England's biggest celebrity: actor David Garrick.

Even for an audacious networker like More, this was an ambitious hope. Over his long and storied career, Garrick had played some of the biggest roles on London's biggest stages, winning the adoration of revelers and royals alike. So it was no big surprise that More didn't stumble upon him at any of the tourist traps she visited in her first few days in the city.

But More had never been one to give up easily.

Walking down the streets of London's affluent Adelphi Terrace, More paid careful attention to the numbers posted above each door, slowing as she reached her destination. Number 5 fell right in the middle of the row of impressive brick homes overlooking the River Thames. This, More had been told, was the home of David Garrick.

With a shaking hand, she knocked on the front door, but the only sound she heard was the pounding of her own heartbeat. A quick conspiratorial glance down the street revealed no watching neighbors, so More, acting before she could talk herself out of it, let herself into the private garden of the most famous man in London.

There, she immediately spotted the actor's legendary chair, "curiously wrought out of a cherry-tree which really grew in the garden of Shakespeare at Stratford."[25] In a letter to a friend, she admitted, "I sat in it, but caught no ray of inspiration."[26]

Upon failing to catch Garrick at his home, More fell back on the tactics that had worked in scoring her an introduction to Thomas Sheridan: poetic praise. After catching Garrick's performance as the titular character of *King Lear*, she rushed back to her rooms to pen a letter to Stonhouse: "Surely [Garrick] is above mortality...His talents are capacious beyond human credibility. I felt myself annihilated before him, and every faculty of my soul was swallowed up in attention."[27]

An amused Stonhouse forwarded the letter to his friend Garrick—the exact outcome More was hoping for.

She would have been delighted to know that when Garrick spotted her name at the bottom of the letter, he recognized it immediately. Her recently published play was gaining attention, and word of her more recent work, *The Inflexible Captive*, was already spreading beyond Bristol, where it was being performed at The Circle.

According to Sally More, "All the world of dukes, lords, and barons were there [in Bristol to see the play]...Never was a piece represented there to have received so much applause. A shout continued for some minutes after the curtain drop."[28]

Garrick had not seen the play, but he'd read it and, upon receiving Stonhouse's forwarded letter, extended an invitation to More to meet him at his home. A few nights later, his coach arrived to pick More up.

David and Eva Garrick were enthralled by their guest from the start. More's "innocent naughtiness lit up her countenance, quiet fun twinkled in her large dark eyes and a slight quirk twisted the corners of her mouth."[29] She was a "touch of fresh air" to a couple who'd spent their lives in the "stuffy atmosphere" of London's elites.[30]

Their evening together proved to be the first of many. Garrick eagerly presented his young writer friend to London's rich and famous, including members of the royal family. As More became the toast of London,

Garrick was filled with pride as if he'd plucked her from the obscurity of Bristol himself.

It was all rather overwhelming for the daughter of a poor schoolteacher, and More often worried that she wouldn't live up to the increasingly high expectations placed on her. After yet another evening of mingling with Garrick's accomplished acquaintances, More confessed, "I felt myself a worm, the more a worm for the consequence which was given me by mixing with such a society."[31]

Despite the social anxiety her upward mobility caused her, More fit in well with the Garricks and their famous friends. With no children of their own, the couple soon began treating More like an adopted daughter and even invited her to live with them, putting an end to her back-and-forth trips between Bristol and London.

Her second-floor room looked out at the River Thames—and the garden where she had once trespassed. It's unknown if she ever confessed to her stolen moments in the Shakespeare chair, but on the night the Garricks gifted her with an inkstand made from the same tree, she must have recalled her escapades with a smile.

Even while living under his roof, More remained an avid fan of Garrick's, watching him perform on stage twenty-seven times in a single season. As he neared the age of retirement, More praised him as "one of those summer suns, which shine brightest at their setting."[32]

Although the Garricks shared More's Christian background, their life on Adelphi Terrace was shaped more by wealth than worship. In one letter to her family, More reported, "I am very well. I eat brown bread and custards like a native; and we have a pretty agreeable, laudable custom of getting tipsy twice a day upon Herefordshire cider."[33] In another, she wrote, "I read four or five hours every day, and wrote ten hours yesterday."[34]

With Garrick right down the hall, invaluable feedback was at the ready. The prolific actor was happy to serve as an early reader, and his extensive stage experience granted him a unique insight that greatly improved her early drafts. And when men of influence criticized More and other women for "making plays [rather than] puddings," Garrick contributed an epilogue for her work in her defense.[35]

With his support, More published the play *Percy* in 1777—and immediately had a smash hit on her hands.

The play ran for twenty-two nights at Garrick's Covent Garden Theater and was met with "bursts of applause" when the curtains fell.[36] Before long, other theaters across England, France, and Austria picked up the play. Four thousand copies of the printed version were sold in just two weeks. When German translations made their way to Vienna, Mozart took special interest in it; a printed copy was found in his personal collection upon his death.

More earned a remarkable six hundred pounds (123,000 US dollars today) in royalties from the work. Under Garrick's tutelage, she had achieved fame and wealth in her own right, but her cushioned lifestyle was not to last. More was about to learn just how fickle fame can be.

CHAPTER 36

I have this moment embraced his coffin, and you come next." Eva Garrick whispered the words to Hannah More in a private embrace, but all of London would soon hear the news: David Garrick was dead.[37]

On February 1, 1779, a procession of more than thirty coaches accompanied Garrick's body from his Adelphi Terrace home to Westminster Abbey for the funeral, where England's royals, rich, and famous presented tickets to be granted entry into the service.

Crowds lined the streets, impervious to the cold. More moved in a daze, impervious to the crowds. As she watched her mentor's body laid to rest in the famous Poets' Corner of the abbey, she muttered in a nod to the book of Job, "This is all of Garrick!…so passes away the fashion of this world."[38]

The next morning, More and Eva Garrick felt the sting of silence as they awoke to a home without their beloved David. It was More's thirty-fourth birthday, but neither felt like celebrating. For the next three months, the pair avoided the public eye—until, on the second night of *The Fatal Falsehood*, Hannah Cowley's pointing finger thrust a reluctant More back into the limelight.

Without Garrick alive to defend her, More was exposed to the unbarred criticisms of the press. "We are tired of indulging Authors because they are Females," complained one journalist, who went on to argue that More's success with *Percy* was only due to "well-timed flattery to a late Manager and Actor."[39]

The character attacks were rather predictable, but still, the slander stung.

More's earliest observations that female playwrights must have the support of an influential man in order to be taken seriously were proving true. Without Garrick's support and friendship, she was unmoored, cast adrift in the shifting tides of public opinion.

Her career may have very well drowned in those tempest-tossed waters if not for an unexpected life preserver placed in her hands in the midst of the storm: a book titled *Cardiphonia*, a collection of letters by Pastor John Newton.

The book seemed written for her from the very first page: "The awakened soul (especially when, after a season of distress and terror, it begins to taste that the Lord is gracious) finds itself as in a new world."[40]

As she poured over the letters, More was enthralled by Newton's faith—a faith he more famously and succinctly described when he wrote, "Amazing grace! How sweet the sound that saved a wretch like me! I once was lost but now am found, was blind but now I see."[41]

More had never fully departed from her Anglican upbringing, but in Newton's writings, she witnessed the life-changing power of a real and personal relationship with one's Savior. The letters were an invitation much like that of the psalmist David: "Taste and see that the LORD is good; blessed is the one who takes refuge in him" (Psalm 34:8).

As she accepted that invitation to taste the Lord's goodness for herself, More began to lose her taste for the life she'd built in London. "The more I see of the 'honoured, famed, and great,'" she wrote, "the more I see…that no earthly pleasure can fill up the wants of the immortal principle within."[42]

The trivialities of wealth began to irk her: "I am annoyed by the foolish absurdity of the present mode of dress. Some ladies carry on their heads a large quantity of fruit, and yet they would despise a poor useful member of society who carried it there for the purpose of selling it for bread."[43]

But through his writings, Newton gave More permission to leave all that behind and embrace a quiet life. In one letter, he wrote that a true Christian would find any calling "honourable and important" because anything done for the purpose of "pleasing his Lord…would be his element and his joy, whether he was appointed to guide the reins of empire, or to sweep the streets."[44]

In another, he praised a friend for retreating from public life altogether, encouraging the friend to devote his days to prayer, reading, and study; to avoid returning to London if at all possible; and to "avoid anything that looks like ostentation, or a desire to be taken notice of" so that his soul might prosper.[45]

In 1785, three years after reading *Cardiphonia* for the first time, More put its advice into action. She bought a humble cottage in rural Cowslip Green and withdrew from London. Life slowed to a peaceful pace as More settled into new rhythms, spending long, slow hours cultivating her garden or exploring "delicious lanes and hills" on horseback.[46]

After two years, More made another audacious attempt at an introduction—but this time, she was looking to further her faith, not her career. She wanted to meet John Newton, the former slave ship captain whose words had changed her life.

After traveling to hear Newton preach, she lingered after the sermon to express her gratitude and then stayed for an hour engaging him in conversation. Back at Cowslip Green, More continued the conversation by letter, detailing the ways God was reshaping her heart and mind: "I have been now some weeks in the quiet enjoyment of my beloved solitude, and the world is wiped out of my memory as with the sponge of oblivion."[47]

With time and distance, her distaste for London only grew:

> When I am in the great world, I consider myself as in an enemy's country, and as beset with snares, and this puts me upon my guard. I know that many people whom I hear say a thousand brilliant and agreeable things disbelieve, or at least disregard, those truths on which I found my everlasting hopes. This sets me upon a more diligent inquiry into those truths; and upon the arch of Christianity, the more I press, the stronger I find it.[48]

But More couldn't stay tucked away in Cowslip Green's rolling hills forever. A culture war was brewing in London, and God was preparing a place for her on the front lines.

CHAPTER 37

When Hannah More escaped to Cowslip Green in 1785, she wasn't London's only celebrity suddenly withdrawing from the public eye. Back in the city, William Wilberforce was also hiding away—and people were beginning to talk.

Twenty-six-year-old Wilberforce was usually the life of the party. After being elected to Parliament at just twenty years old, he'd quickly won over London's rich and famous with his quick wit and magnetic charm. Most nights, he could be found drinking, singing, and gambling until morning at the city's most exclusive gentlemen's clubs.

But that all changed when, after a rich discussion with a friend, Wilberforce came face-to-face with a truth he'd been avoiding for years: The God he'd learned about as a child was real, Jesus was God, and the truth of the Scriptures meant there was more to life than partying and power.

Ashamed of how he'd lived and unsure of what to do next, Wilberforce abruptly resigned from all his usual social clubs and began hiding away at home in isolation. People began to wonder if he'd gone "melancholy mad."[49]

Unsure of where else to turn, Wilberforce went in secret to visit the man who had once been like a father to him: Pastor John Newton. Their conversation would change the world forever.

Newton listened carefully to Wilberforce's anxious fears that every decision he'd ever made had been wrong, that the only way to follow the God he now believed in wholeheartedly was to withdraw from politics and enter the priesthood.

By God's grace, Newton didn't repeat the advice that he'd penned to the friend in *Cardiphonia*—advice that, at that very moment, was the reason Hannah More was resting her head in a tiny country cottage away from London.

Instead, prompted by the Holy Spirit, Newton urged Wilberforce to stay right where he was: "Who knew—his reasoning went—but that Wilberforce had been prepared 'for such a time as this'? Who knew but that God would use him mightily in the world of politics, where he was needed more than ever?"[50]

Wilberforce listened and began to cautiously, prayerfully reenter London society, constantly seeking the Lord for guidance. And so, for the next two years, Wilberforce followed Newton's advice to seek God in the city while More followed the same man's advice to seek God in the country.

Then, in the fall of 1787, Newton's two young friends met over dinner. More took an instant liking to Wilberforce: "That young man's character is one of the most extraordinary I have ever known for talent, virtue, and piety. It is difficult not to grow better and wiser every time one converses with him."[51]

And in More, Wilberforce found a rare treasure: a like-minded Christian and intellectual equal with whom he could wrestle through the many theological and cultural questions that kept him up at night. After one dinner, More recorded that she had enjoyed "four or five hours of most confidential and instructive conversation [with Wilberforce], in which we discussed all the great objects of reform."[52]

As they talked about the cultural issues of the day, the new friends came to agree on one issue as more urgent than the rest. The horrors of slavery— which, they knew, formed the economic bedrock of the country they called home—were in direct opposition to their Christian faith and the inherent dignity of people made in the image of God.

Shortly after meeting More, Wilberforce famously journaled, "God Almighty has set before me two great objects, the suppression of the slave trade and the reformation of manners."[53]

More's letter to a friend at around the same time reveals her similar commitment to what she called "the great object I have so much at heart,—the project to abolish the slave-trade in Africa."[54]

Together, and with God's help, More and Wilberforce hatched a plan. Wilberforce would dedicate his political career to the cause of abolition while More would dedicate her pen to the very same cause. "You know enough of life," Wilberforce told More, "to be aware that in parliamentary measures of importance, more is to be done out of the House than in it."[55]

Very few British people had ever been exposed to the horrific realities of the slave trade. What was out of sight remained out of mind. So before Wilberforce could change the minds of his fellow legislators, he knew he would need More's help to stir people's hearts for the cause.

More, who had always believed in the power of the written word, jumped at the opportunity to leverage her talents for a Name far greater than her own. Her first contribution was a poem simply titled "Slavery," and all 2,660 words of it were crafted to convict.

She opened by arguing that England was mired in hypocrisy ("She raves of mercy, while she deals out death") and that the economic benefits of slavery could never justify its means:

> Whene'er to Afric's shores I turn my eyes,
> Horrors of deepest, deadliest guilt arise;
> I see, by more than Fancy's mirror shown,
> The burning village, and the blazing town:
> See the dire victim torn from social life,
> See the sacred infant, hear the shrieking wife!
> She, wretch forlorn! is dragged by hostile hands,
> To distant tyrants sold, in distant lands:
> Transmitted miseries, and successive chains,
> The sole sad heritage her child obtains.

But More reserved her sharpest jabs for self-proclaiming Christians who misrepresented the heart of their Creator to the African people:

> Sullen, he mingles with his kindred dust,
> For he has learned to dread the Christian's trust;
> To him what mercy can that God display,
> Whose servants murder, and whose sons betray?[56]

The poem was just the beginning. More quickly became the chief mastermind in what amounted to the world's first marketing campaign for the cause of abolition, urging fellow creatives to join her in the fight. Under her leadership, the topic of slavery was tackled in poetry, pamphlets, and plays that suddenly took London by storm.

Back in Bristol, John Wesley asked More's sister to pass on a message: "Tell

[Hannah] to live in the world; there is the sphere of her usefulness; they will not let us [pastors] come nigh them."[57]

He was right. More knew she couldn't hide away in the sleepy pastures of Cowslip Green any longer. It was time to return to London.

CHAPTER 38

When Hannah More returned to London a few years after *Slavery* went to print, she wasn't thinking about bishops and booksellers or even publishers and performers. This time, she was going to visit the abolitionists and activists gathered at Battersea Rise.

Just a few miles from London, the sprawling mansion was more headquarters than haven, a place where devoted Christians agreed to not isolate from culture but insulate with one another while strategizing ways they might bring God's kingdom to earth.

Standing in the home's legendary Oval Library, Hannah More could barely contain her excitement. The meetings held in this room were always full of passionate discussion about big ideas to further causes such as abolition, but today was special. Today, the big idea was hers.

As the meeting time drew near, the room began to fill with members of what would come to be known as the Clapham Community. Some were clergymen or missionaries, but many, including More's friend William Wilberforce, were mere Christians working in government, banking, business, and mathematics.

More kicked off the meeting by passing around the paperback "tracts" she'd been buying up from street vendors around London. Much like a magazine, each tract featured various short stories, superstitious tales, and bawdy song lyrics.

Such a lowbrow form of literature was generally considered beneath the educated people gathered in the room. More, however, had become a voracious reader of the tracts—not, as everyone was about to learn, to engage with them as a consumer. She had been studying them as a marketer, seeking to reverse-engineer why these tracts were flying off the shelves.

As copies were passed around the room, More presented her idea: What if they produced their own tracts as a way to spread their abolitionist messages? Many working-class Londoners were just learning to read, and they'd never use their limited spare time to wrestle with a theological tome. But these short paperbacks had already proven popular in the marketplace. Why not redeem the medium for their own causes?

The activists scattered around the library leafed through the tracts, contrasting them in their minds with More's most recent book, which had spread like wildfire among London's elite. Everyone from royals to bishops was clamoring for copies. When Queen Victoria found within it More's criticisms of wealthy ladies who expected their hairdressers to work on Sundays, she declared, "She is in the right, and I will never send for one again."[58]

In the book's first three months, publishers were forced to print seven editions, some of which sold out within just a few hours. But More was right: No one in the working classes was buying or reading it.

Sensing the interest in the Oval Library, More began outlining her plan in more detail. She'd give each tract a tantalizing title and then hire one of the city's best engravers to make original, eye-catching covers that would stand out on street vendor's crowded shelves.

Inside, readers would find everything from poems and hymns to recipes and money-saving tips. But most of all, they would find stories—stories that introduced them to a Christian perspective in general and the abolitionist cause specifically.

Heads in the room nodded in excitement. Ideas like this were exactly what they'd come to expect from More. Ever since the publication of her poem *Slavery*, More had been masterminding a charge to encourage Christian creatives to use their gifts for the glory of God and the good of others. But this idea could expand their reach to entirely new social groups.

It would also further both of the group's two central goals: "One, to promote true religion and save souls; the other, to make life better for people and to make the world a better place. Neither was merely the means to the other; both were essential; both were, as they understood it, the work of God."[59]

More's project gained so much financial support from those in the Clapham Community that she was able to move forward and even sell the tracts at a loss to further her goals of mass production and widespread readership.

The strategy was an instant success. From March 1795 through September 1798, More oversaw the production of more than one hundred issues of the tracts. And despite printing two million copies in less than a year, publishers struggled to keep up with demand.

The sales were largely due to More's talents as a storyteller and marketer. By employing groundbreaking literary techniques, such as cliffhangers and crossover events, More kept readers perennially excited to buy the next tract in the series. As a result, she exposed countless Londoners—many for the first time—to stories that portrayed Africans as people with inherent value, human longings, and deep sorrows as a result of the gut-wrenching realities of slavery.

There were reports of at least one reader coming to Christ after reading More's tracts, and the "astonishing moral change" that swept the culture led William Wilberforce to credit her work with turning the tides of public opinion against slavery.[60]

But More would never see the project—or the credit—as hers alone. She'd come to understand that her best work was accomplished not alone but alongside like-minded believers in Clapham.

In community, she could engage the world without falling for its traps of fame and glory. And from community, she could venture into territories no one else had dared to go.

CHAPTER 39

The red-faced farmer sitting across from Hannah More and her sister Martha belched loudly. He didn't care that the two ladies at his rough-hewn table had just walked on foot the ten unpaved miles from Cowslip Green. And he sure didn't care that one of them had once been "courted and caressed…half-worshipped" by London's upper classes more than a hundred miles away.[61]

Here in the village of Cheddar, he was as good as king, and if the women wanted to do anything in his town, they'd have to get him on board first.

Influenced by her involvement with the Clapham Community in London, Hannah More had come to view her country cottage at Cowslip Green as an opportunity for revival rather than retreat. With help from her sisters and friends, she developed a plan to bring hope to communities where no one else dared to go: the rural villages dotted across the English countryside.

The plan, as she explained to the farmer, was to open a school in the countryside town of Cheddar. Since most children had to work six days a week alongside their parents on his farm or in dangerous mines, stone quarries, and factories, the school would meet for just a few hours a week on their day off. These "Sunday Schools" would use a Bible-based curriculum to teach villagers how to read and write.

The farmer's response was swift and harsh. "He begged I would not think of bringing any religion into the country; it was the worst thing in the world for the poor, for it made them lazy and useless," More recounted in a letter to William Wilberforce.[62]

More tried reassuring the farmer—surely a Christian education would only lead the families employed by him to "be more industrious, as they were better principled."[63] But the counterargument only sent the man into further rage.

Exchanging a meaningful glance with her sister, More deftly switched topics and tactics: "We were obliged prudently to change the subject, and talk of the excellency of his wine, as though we had been soliciting a vote at an election. This put him into good humour," as did the sisters' reassurance that they already had funding for their school and wanted nothing from him except for his consent to engage his employees on their day off.[64]

As the wine flowed and dinner was served, the Mores began to feel they had "gained ground" with the "ignorant, cold, unfeeling rich farmer."[65] By the time they said their goodbyes, the women were cautiously optimistic that they could move forward with their plan to start a school nearby.

The school would be the first of its kind. No one had ever deemed rural children of the working poor worthy of an education, and most gave small towns like Cheddar a wide berth.

"Drunkenness and indolence prevailed in almost every cottage," observed More. Although rural villages often featured picturesque hills and scenic cliffs, word of the "rioting and debauchery" that took place at would-be travel destinations kept visitors far away.[66]

"The sacred Sabbath was regularly profaned by scenes exhibited in the cliffs, too shocking and indelicate to be named here," wrote More. "Strangers were sometimes assaulted…A creditable woman told me herself, her life was endangered whilst walking quietly through the cliffs, with a few friends, and the virtue of her companions dreadfully assaulted."[67]

Even the clergy assigned to the villages by the Church of England chose to live so far from their parishes that they generally made appearances only to extract tithes from the community. And if they did show up to preach, very few showed up to listen. Even in villages with hundreds of families, More found that "five women and fifteen men were no unusual number to compose a morning congregation."[68]

"We saw but one Bible in all [of Cheddar]," lamented More, "and that was used to prop a flower pot."[69]

Drawing from their experience in their successful private school, the More sisters set about securing a building for rent, hiring a teacher, and training her in a Bible-based curriculum.

On the school's opening day, More recorded a full account for Wilberforce: "The church was crowded; it had never been remembered so full…for forty years." The villagers had been exchanging stories of how "two ladies came and made many inquiries about the poor, and talked about setting up a school," but they were all shocked to find that unlike the unreliable clergymen who had come before them, the Mores actually "did all they said they would."[70]

Within weeks, the small Cheddar school more than doubled from 140 to 300 enrolled children.

When Hannah More came to observe the students' progress five weeks after opening day, she found that "upwards of thirty said the Catechism perfectly, forty could sing three psalms, and several great girls were beginning to know something of the Scriptures."[71]

Beyond the classroom, she found "the face of the village much changed; not a child to be found on the cliffs on a Sunday; the church gradually filling." Before long, the church that had once averaged a dozen men in attendance on any given Sunday swelled to a congregation of five hundred adults squeezing into pews newly built to accommodate the growth.[72]

Invigorated by the miraculous transformation they were witnessing, the More sisters decided to replicate the Sunday School model in as many rural villages as possible.

Sometimes, the work brought measurable progress and great joy—like the annual celebrations where thousands would gather on rolling green hills to eat "as much as their stomachs would hold" and hear the students recite Bible passages they'd memorized.[73] Those days felt like glimpses of heaven, and villagers would recount the memories for generations to come.

But most days were far less glamorous. Hannah More, who had once passed her days lounging around with books and cider, now found herself traveling up to twenty miles a day on horseback and foot to visit the schools she'd established.

On nights when darkness fell fast and hard with miles of dangerous, rural roads still stretched ahead of them, it could be hard to believe the work was worth it. But then the sun would rise on another day, and More would sit down to capture the Lord's faithfulness in her journal.

"The good providence of God has preserved us from evil, and gives us strength and faith to persevere," she wrote. "Oh, may we never be restrained by fear or self-love, when any good is to be done!"[74]

Over the next thirty years, the "good to be done" would exceed even the audacious Hannah More's wildest imagination. Thousands of poor children would come through her Sunday Schools, learn to read the Bible, and share what they learned with their families, slowly changing the culture of entire villages.

Eventually, other educators would follow in More's footsteps. Within a few decades, three out of four of England's working-class children were enrolled in Sunday Schools, which ultimately evolved into the country's modern-day public school system.

But even as More made great strides with England's poorest children, her thoughts were often with the children she couldn't reach: the children of African slaves. The fight for abolition had still not been won.

CHAPTER 40

Gazing up at the leafy green branches overhead, Hannah More let out a deep, contented sigh. Her primary residence was still the tiny cottage at Cowslip Green one mile away, but in her heart, she knew this uncultivated plot of land she'd just purchased would soon be her new home.

As she walked the grounds, she could see it in her mind's eye as clear as any story that had ever bid her to sit and write.

Here, she thought, would mark the entrance to the house: a sprawling, Georgian-style house with plenty of room for all four sisters to live with her. And there would be the terrace, opening up with a stunning view of idyllic green fields, bordered neatly by trees. And over there would be her gardens, where she'd spend a long, happy retirement, passing slow, peaceful days with her hands in the dirt and her mind on the Lord.

She could hardly wait.

Construction progressed quickly while More busied herself with her growing network of Sunday Schools, and in 1801, her home was ready for her to move in. The home, which she called Barley Wood, perfectly matched the vision she'd held. The life she lived there, however, would not quite follow her blueprints.

Even at nearly sixty years of age, More would find she simply couldn't turn off the calling the Lord had given her to meet the needs around her. Although she'd still find time to work in the gardens she'd love, her "retirement" was going to prove even busier than the years preceding it.

Over the coming years, Barley Wood's nine bedrooms would be perpetually filled with a rotating cast of friends, clergymen, and fans of her work. On at least one occasion, More welcomed eighty visitors in a single week. On another, she hosted a party where "a hundred and one sat down to dinner, and about one hundred and sixty to tea." When the home itself was full, the dinner party spilled out on the lawn where "above fifty dined under the trees… They all enjoyed themselves exceedingly."[75]

When William Wilberforce visited, he and More would talk for hours of their now lifelong fight for abolition, a conversation they continued by letters whenever they were apart. Wilberforce kept More abreast of his efforts in Parliament, while More would report on the devotional books she was writing to, she hoped, stir people's hearts toward holiness.

But time was passing quickly, and both knew they were getting older. Would they even live to see the abolition for which they'd labored and prayed?

In 1813, the tight-knit circle of More sisters was rocked by the death of their eldest sister Mary. Over the next nine years, in rapid succession, each of More's remaining sisters—and most of her closest friends—passed away.

By the time she was seventy-seven years old, only Wilberforce remained. "I am feeling the common effect of those who live to an advanced age," More lamented in a letter to her last living friend. "Almost all my contemporaries are dropping before me."[76]

Eventually, More's own declining health made it impossible for her to live alone at her beloved Barley Wood any longer. When a carriage arrived to take her away, More descended from her upstairs bedroom with an air of poise and solemnity.

As the coachman waited outside, More took a silent stroll through the home once filled with life and laughter. Every few steps, she paused to gaze at "the walls…covered with the portraits of all her old and dear friends, who had successively gone before her."[77]

Finally, it was time to go. Stepping up into the carriage, More cast a final, longing glance over her shoulder and remarked, "I am driven like Eve out of Paradise."[78] It was the end of an era—but not, she knew, the end of her life.

At eighty-eight years of age, More could no longer write for the cause of abolition, but she could still pray: "Prayer was the last thing that lived in her," observed one visitor; "every breath was prayer."[79]

In July 1833, the news reached a homebound More that one of her biggest prayers had been answered. The Slavery Abolition Act had passed Parliament unopposed. When a visiting acquaintance praised More for her good works toward that end, More replied, "Talk not so vainly, I utterly cast [any good works] from me, and fall low at the foot of the cross."[80] The victory, she knew, was the Lord's.

One week later, the joy was tinged with sorrow at the news that her dear friend William Wilberforce had died. But just two months later, on September 7, 1833, More joined the friends and family she loved in the presence of the one she loved most, her Lord and Savior Jesus Christ. Her final days were full of peace and prayer, her last word a simple exclamation with outstretched arms: "Joy!"[81]

Bells rang out over Bristol as two hundred children led the funeral procession to the church, followed by landowning nobility, humble country folk, and solemn clergymen.

The little girl who'd once dreamed of meeting the culture-making bishops and booksellers of London had become "the most influential woman of her time."[82] Historians would call her "the first Victorian" for sparking a cultural change so sweeping that it birthed the beginning of a new era marked by a commitment to religious and moral values.[83] And missionaries would name several generations of orphaned girls freed from slavery "Hannah More" in her honor.

Hand in hand with God and fellow Christians, Hannah More had embarked on audacious adventures that took her from her country's most elite social circles to rural villages where no one else dared to go.

And while the journey was not always easy and the gratification was rarely, if ever, instant, any mere Christian longing to follow in her faithful footsteps will do well to remember this: Joy was hers to the very last.

THREE WAYS TO GLORIFY GOD IN YOUR WORK
AS SEEN IN THE LIFE OF HANNAH MORE

Even though she's the oldest of five mere Christians in this book, I (Jordan) would argue that Hannah More's story is the most relevant in this current cultural moment. At a time when Christians are increasingly tempted to retreat from "secular" workplaces and culture at large, More shows us a better, more Jesus-like way. Here are three specific ways you and I can glorify God in our work today as illustrated by the life of Hannah More.

I. MERE CHRISTIANS GLORIFY GOD BY REJECTING ISOLATION AND EMBRACING INSULATION.

Jesus said, "Let your light shine before others, that they may see your good deeds and glorify your Father in heaven" (Matthew 5:16). But lights don't shine in already-bright places. They shine in the dark. Which is why, just before his death, Jesus pleaded with the Father on our behalf saying, "My prayer is not that you take them out of the world...As you sent me into the world, I have sent them into the world" (John 17:15-18).

Sadly, many Christians are fighting against Jesus's prayer today. I know *so* many believers who only want to work for Christian employers, send their kids to Christian schools, and consume exclusively Christian content. To be clear, there is nothing wrong with any one of these decisions. But in aggregate, they point to a disturbing trend of retreat and isolation from the world that stands in stark contrast to Jesus's call on our lives.

By God's grace, Hannah More came to reject this type of isolation—but not at first. As a young believer, More initially made plans to abandon her "secular" work, retreat from the worldly temptations of London, and isolate herself in the countryside at Cowslip Green.

That's when William Wilberforce and other believers intervened, showing More that, as she would later write, "Mischief…arises not from our living in the world, but from the world living in us; occupying our hearts, and monopolizing our affections."[84] Eventually, More came to a place of rejecting *isolation* from the world while embracing *insulation* that would enable her to be in the world but not of it.

Think about the insulation a jacket provides for a moment. A jacket insulates you from the cold *so that you can engage it*—so that you can be "in the cold but not of the cold," if you will. We need something similar for the Christian life. Like Hannah More, we will glorify God by rejecting isolation from the world and yet ensuring that we are properly insulated to engage the darkness that surrounds us. What does that look like practically?

First, *be in God's Word*. Right after Jesus asked the Father not to take his followers "out of the world," he prayed that God would "protect" us as we lived in the world. How? Jesus prayed, "Sanctify them by the truth; your word is truth" (see John 17:15-17). Scripture is your first line of insulation from the world.

Here's the second: *Be in a local church*. There has been a lot of debate about the importance of the local church in recent years. Personally, I can't get around the strong biblical case for insulating with a local body of believers (see Hebrews 10:24–25).

Finally, *be in community with other mere Christians*. It is highly unlikely that Hannah More would have had the impact she did had she *only* been involved in a local church. She needed Wilberforce and the Clapham Community: a group of serious, high-achieving Christian professionals who understood her ambition, idols, and nuances of her craft. She needed a community that could engage thoughtfully in theological discussions *and* strategic ones.

You and I need the same type of community today. That could take the form of a Christian employee resource group at your large company, a small group you organize of other believers in your profession, or something like the online Mere Christians Community I have the privilege of leading at jordanraynor.com/mcc.

Find whatever works for you, believer. But insulate we must. Because you and I are called not to flee from the world but to shine within it, allowing our presence—like Hannah More's—to reflect the Light of the World amid the present darkness.

2. MERE CHRISTIANS GLORIFY GOD BY ADVANCING HIS KINGDOM CULTURALLY AND NOT JUST POLITICALLY.

Political change is one of the chief idols of the American church today. We think that if we simply vote the "right people" into office, they will appoint the "right judges" to legislate our flavor of change and that God's kingdom will finally come on earth as it is in heaven.

This rationale is seriously flawed and ironic for two reasons.

First, *Jesus himself advanced God's kingdom through culture, not politics.* He didn't seek out a political post on the Jewish Sanhedrin or in the Roman Senate. He sat by the seaside telling stories to the masses. Jesus changed the world through not politics but parables—tiny tales that artistically made people long for God's kingdom.

Second, *historically, cultural change has almost always preceded political change.* Take the fight for abolition in the United States as a case in point. The beginning of the end of slavery in America was not Lincoln's Emancipation Proclamation but *Uncle Tom's Cabin.* When Lincoln met Harriet Beecher Stowe, the author of the massively popular novel, he said, "So, you're the little woman who wrote the book that made this great war."[85]

And of course, we saw cultural change precede political change in the life of Hannah More.

Given the political idolatry of our day, it is not surprising that William Wilberforce receives the lion's share of credit for abolishing the slave trade across the British Empire. And while Wilberforce certainly deserves much respect and admiration for the part that he played, historians and Wilberforce himself give More equal credit.

Eric Metaxas, a biographer of both Wilberforce and More, says, "How Wilberforce came to be the chief champion of abolition...*has everything to do with Hannah More.*"[86] Had More not first changed people's hearts toward the issue of slavery in her cultural works of poems, novels, and tracts, legislative change would likely have never happened.

Metaxas goes on to argue that Hannah More's story should serve as "a corrective to the idea that the only way to effect change in the world is via political action...It is true that we can always use another Wilberforce...but what we need far more is another Hannah More."[87]

Can Christians glorify God by advancing his kingdom through politics? Of course. But we *also* glorify him when we work to advance his kingdom through culture.

What might this look like practically today? Let's take the issue of abortion as a case study. Murder has no place in the kingdom of God. So when we see the practice of abortion, it is right to ask the question, "What is the *political* response to this problem?" But the far more powerful question is, "What is my *creative* response to this problem?"

If you're an artist like Hannah More, your response might be to write stories and songs that break people's hearts toward orphans and birth parents. If you're a business leader, your response could be the creation of uncommonly generous paid maternity and paternity policies or a program that funds adoptions for your team. If you work in a café, you may feel called to create a community board and post information for local pregnancy centers.

My point is this: Whenever you see something at odds with God's kingdom—abortion, racial injustice, gender transitioning, pollution, and so on—glorify God not just by working to change things politically but first and foremost culturally. Because in the words of author Andy Crouch, "The only way to change culture is to create more of it."[88]

3. MERE CHRISTIANS GLORIFY GOD BY LIVING WITH UNCOMMON AUDACITY.

The moment I read about Hannah More showing up unannounced at the home of England's biggest celebrity, I knew I *had* to tell this woman's story.

Why? Because I believe God is honored by holy and humble audacity—and Hannah More had it in spades.

This woman was shamelessly pitching her plays to the world's most famous actors in her early twenties. She started schools for the poor in the face of opposition from angry and powerful employers. She had the audacity to believe that she could help *abolish the slave trade* in her lifetime. And let's not forget that More demonstrated this otherworldly boldness *as a single woman in the eighteenth century.*

Like Hannah More, mere Christians today should be the most audacious people on the planet. Why? Because God promises that he "is able to do immeasurably more than all we ask or imagine" through us (see Ephesians 3:20).

Now, this is not a license to chase after "immeasurably more" possessions. It's a call to believe that God is able to do far more than you can imagine for *his* glory and the good of *others* through *you*, his willing servant.

Furthermore, you and I should be uncommonly bold in our work and lives because we of all people have nothing ultimate to lose. Even when we fail in our audacious pursuits, nothing "will be able to separate us from the love of God that is in Christ Jesus our Lord" (see Romans 8:38-39).

You and I will glorify God when—in response to those truths—we live with uncommon boldness for his purposes in the world. How can we begin to imitate Hannah More's audacity today?

First, *write down the audacious thing you would pursue if you* actually *believed the biblical truths above.*

Second, *write down the worst-case scenario if you pursue that audacious goal and fail.* And remember that even in *total* failure (which is very unlikely), you will still be an adopted child of God.

Finally, *share your audacious dream with another believer* who can check your motives and help you discern whether you are pursuing this bold vision for your glory or God's.

The same Holy Spirit that lived inside Hannah More lives inside you, believer. I pray that truth inspires you to live with otherworldly audacity— driven not by a desire for *your* good and *your* glory but a desire to do immeasurably more for the glory of God and the good of others.

PART V

C.S. LEWIS

AUTHOR OF *THE CHRONICLES OF NARNIA*

HOW TO GLORIFY GOD BY PURSUING JOY PROPERLY, CREATING
KINGDOM CRAVINGS, AND PROCLAIMING CHRIST BOLDLY

On August 6, 1941, a world leader and a college professor each readied himself to speak up in service of a nation in crisis. British prime minister Winston Churchill, preparing for a secret meeting with Franklin D. Roosevelt, was already a household name. C.S. Lewis, making his way to the BBC broadcasting offices, was about to become one.

For the past two years, Great Britain had been fighting a desperate war against evil, and evil was clearly winning. The Germans and the Japanese were forging paths of horror across the globe, and from September 1940 to May 1941, Nazi pilots bombed London nearly every night.

British citizens carried gas masks to church and wore identification bracelets everywhere they went so someone could notify their family if they were "blown into unidentifiable pieces."[1] And that was one of the more merciful ways to go.

Almost 29,000 citizens died, and nearly as many were seriously injured in this air attack known as "the Blitz." Death and terror loomed large for citizens of all ages. When a young London boy was asked what he wanted to be when he grew up, he flatly replied, "Alive."[2]

Churchill wanted nothing more than to defeat Hitler and protect his people, but he knew he couldn't do so without the help of the United States. For over a year, he'd sent increasingly desperate letters to President Roosevelt but seemed to be making no progress at all.

"The best of luck to you," Roosevelt signed off in one particularly maddening response.[3]

And it wasn't just the American president who was failing to come through for Great Britain. Many citizens thought God Almighty seemed equally deaf to their cries. Didn't he see how dire things were? Didn't he care?

Those were the questions C.S. Lewis was invited to answer in a BBC broadcast on the evening of Wednesday, August 6, 1941, at the same time that Churchill was preparing for a secret sit-down with President Roosevelt aboard the USS *Augusta*.

Despite his preparation and desperation, Churchill's meeting would prove unsuccessful. America wouldn't declare war until Japan's attack on Pearl Harbor four months later.

At the time, Lewis also seemed set up to fail. His time slot was just fifteen minutes—not nearly long enough to address the existential questions of a traumatized nation. Besides, it was unlikely anyone would be tuned in to hear him try. His broadcast would follow a news update in Norwegian that would prompt most English-speaking listeners to switch their radios off for the evening.

At the very moment C.S. Lewis was sitting down behind a microphone at the BBC, a Royal Air Force officer was sitting at a bar across town with the weight of a war on his shoulders. He flagged down a bartender for another pint. Just as the bartender extended a glass of beer in the officer's direction, a rich, booming voice cut through the murmured conversations in the room.

"Everyone has heard people quarreling," the voice said. "'That's my seat, I was there first.' 'Leave him alone, he isn't doing you any harm.' 'Why should you shove me in first?' 'Give me a bit of your orange, I gave you a bit of mine.' 'How'd you like it if anyone did the same to you?' 'Come on, you promised.'"[4]

The voice was that of C.S. Lewis, broadcasting live from the BBC on a radio no one had bothered to turn off.

"Suddenly everyone just froze listening to this extraordinary voice and what he had to say," recalled another officer in the bar. "And finally they end up and there was the barman with his arm still up there and the other man still waiting for his drink. And they all forgot it, so riveting was that [talk by C.S. Lewis]."[5]

Time stood still for listeners as Lewis passionately yet methodically laid out his case that (a) there is evidence of a universal moral law, (b) we all disobey it, and (c) the "existence of a Lawgiver is at least very probable."[6]

When it was over, the bar resumed its normal hum of activity. The officer finally accepted his drink. And the radio continued with its regularly scheduled programming as Lewis caught a train back home. A war-weary nation had just gotten a glimpse of another kingdom, and the world would never be the same.

Lewis's broadcast that night was just the first in a five-week series. With each passing week, growing audiences gathered around radios in pubs and living rooms. Soon, and to the surprise of many, these talks on morality and the meaning of the universe catapulted C.S. Lewis into bona fide fame. He became a household name first in Great Britain and then around the world.

In 1952, those radio broadcasts were compiled in a book titled *Mere Christianity*. In 2000, *Christianity Today* declared that book the number one religious book of the twentieth century, and another four million copies have sold since.

But Lewis's broadcasts weren't sermons, and he was certainly no clergyman—which is exactly why he was handed a microphone in the first place.

"I think [the BBC] asked me chiefly for two reasons: firstly, because I am a layman, not a clergyman," Lewis explained later. "And secondly, because I had been a non-Christian for many years. It was thought that both these facts might enable me to understand the difficulties that ordinary people feel about the subject."[7]

The BBC was right on both points. By selecting a mere Christian for the talks, the station was able to sidestep religious politics while offering a fresh, approachable perspective on the spiritual questions of a terrified and grieving audience.

And by selecting C.S. Lewis in particular, they found someone who understood what it was like to be an estranged son, a teenage pleasure seeker, a scared soldier, an adamant atheist, an alleged adulterer, and an ambitious professional. It's no wonder Lewis sounded like a trusted friend to so many.

But Lewis's story is not just riveting; it's also highly relevant to us today. It's a story that shows how mere Christians like you can glorify God by finding your ultimate joy in Christ alone, scratching off glimpses of God's kingdom through your seemingly secular work, and embracing your job outside of the church as an ideal forum for making disciples of Jesus Christ.

And it's a story that reminds us all that our ordinary work, when done with and unto God, holds extraordinary potential beyond our wildest dreams.

CHAPTER 42

Childhood was idyllic, cozy, and safe for C.S. Lewis—until it wasn't.

Born in Ireland on November 29, 1898, Clive Staples Lewis (who preferred to be called "Jack" throughout his life) was raised in a Christian home. His father, Albert, practiced law. His mother, Flora, was the college-educated daughter of a chaplain, the branches of her family tree filled with clergymen.

The family attended St. Mark's Anglican Church on the outskirts of Belfast. Each time they attended a service, young Jack passed by a "door knocker in the form of a lion's head," its full mane and kind eyes not unlike those Lewis would give Aslan many years later.[8]

"I was taught the usual things and made to say my prayers and in due time taken to church," Lewis later reflected. "I naturally accepted what I was told but I cannot remember feeling much interest in [Christianity]."[9]

In his early years, Jack wasn't shaped by his family's faith so much as his country's weather. Often trapped indoors by Ireland's incessant rain, he and his big brother Warnie were forced to entertain themselves within the four walls of their childhood home, known affectionately as "Little Lea."

"I am a product of long corridors, empty sunlit rooms, upstair indoor silences, attics explored in solitude, distant noises of gurgling cisterns and pipes, and the noise of wind under the tiles. Also, of endless books," he later recalled with fondness.[10]

When the brothers tired of reading, they dreamed up stories of their own. In an imaginary land they called Boxen, talking animals embarked on exciting adventures through strange kingdoms. Even as a young boy, Jack longed to bring his imaginary world to life. But he quickly discovered the infuriating gap that can span between the image in one's mind and the creation of one's hands.

"I longed to make things, ships, houses, engines. Many sheets of cardboard and pairs of scissors I spoiled, only to turn from my hopeless failures in tears," he wrote. "As a last resource…I was driven to write stories instead; little dreaming to what a world of happiness I was being admitted. You can do more with a castle in a story than with the best cardboard castle that ever stood on a nursery table."[11]

Elements of those early childhood stories would ultimately live on in his most famous work, *The Lion, the Witch and the Wardrobe*. The story opens with the four Pevensie children waking up, just like Jack and Warnie often did, to "a steady rain falling, so thick that when you looked out of the window you could see neither the mountains nor the woods nor even the stream in the garden."[12]

It's their first day as evacuees from the bombing in London, and they're staying in an eccentric professor's rambling mansion. As they set off to investigate its winding staircases, long passages, and never-ending rooms, young Lucy lags behind, drawn in by a wardrobe filled with furs. It is there that she discovers a magical land called Narnia just begging to be explored.

Much like the Pevensies, the Lewis brothers often embarked on grand, rainy-day adventures without ever leaving home. Of course, even a country as lush and green as Ireland experiences a break in the rain every once in a while. And it was on one of those rare sunshiny days that Jack's brother Warnie wandered out to play in the family's garden.

As he explored, he gathered bits of moss, twigs, and flowers, as little boys are inclined to do. Then, crouched down in the grass, he carefully arranged his collection into a miniature garden in the lid of a cookie tin. With slow, intentional steps and a firm but careful grip on his tiny creation, Warnie returned inside to give Jack his handiwork. Jack was awed, as little brothers are inclined to be.

It was the first time Jack was stirred to deep joy, a feeling he'd later come to view as a glimpse of eternity, much like a hidden passageway to Narnia. "As long as I live my imagination of Paradise will retain something of my brother's toy garden," he later wrote.[13]

But feelings, like childhoods, are fleeting. This picturesque boyhood, with its cozy cottage full of books and brotherly adventures, was about to slip through Lewis's fingers. His father would uproot young Jack at the worst possible moment. He would lose everyone and everything he loved. And his faith wouldn't survive it.

CHAPTER 43

Nine-year-old Jack wanted his mother. Lying in bed with a toothache he could no longer ignore, he cried out for her, longing for her comforting touch and reassuring voice. Despite his tears and pain, she didn't come, and he couldn't understand why.

Six months prior, Flora Lewis had experienced some nagging pains of her own. Jack's father Albert called a doctor, who came for a home visit and diagnosed Flora with cancer. It was February of 1908. There would be no CT scans, no chemotherapy, and no cancer specialists to help her beat the odds.

One week after her diagnosis, a small team of doctors and nurses performed surgery on Flora right in the Lewis home. Jack, able to hear everything from the next room, was terrified.

The treatment—and her youngest son's fervent prayers—seemed to work, at least for a time. Flora even felt well enough to take Jack on a seaside vacation in May. But just a few weeks later, she was bedridden once again.

Lying in her room for weeks on end, Flora was forced to face a gut-wrenching reality. She was running out of time to impart everything she longed to share with her sons. She begged Albert to go out and purchase two Bibles. If she couldn't be there to give her sons comfort, she desperately hoped they would discover it in the pages of God's Word after she was gone.

Then, on August 23, 1908, as Jack cried out for her from his bed, Flora slipped away from him in hers. That she was stepping into eternity and healing was of little comfort to a nine-year-old facing a toothache and the end of his idyllic childhood.

As he later recalled, "With my mother's death all settled happiness, all that was tranquil and reliable, disappeared from my life."[14]

Albert, completely overwhelmed by his own grief, faced a decision. What was he going to do with two little boys who'd just lost their mother? Staring blankly out the window, he would have seen the shipyards across from the family home. His sons loved watching the massive hulls take shape under the capable hands of the builders.

That was, he decided, what his boys needed: capable hands to shape them into men. Feeling completely unequipped to do the job himself, he resolved to send young Jack off to boarding school in England.

He and Flora had already sent Warnie to boarding school, where he seemed to be doing well. And they'd always intended to send Jack eventually, Albert reasoned. What would it hurt to send him a few years earlier than expected?

And so, just two weeks after Flora's death, "an emotionally unintelligent father bade his emotionally neglected sons an emotionally inadequate farewell" as he put them on an overnight steamer to England—completely and utterly alone.[15]

Unfortunately, even professionals can make devastating, life-altering missteps. The seemingly capable builders in the nearby shipyard would soon begin construction on the *Titanic*. And across the Irish Sea, Jack was embarking on an ill-fated journey of his own.

When he arrived at Wynyard School in Hertfordshire, England, Jack was desperately in need of love and guidance. Instead, he was met with an abusive headmaster "whose chief delight seemed to be flogging the boys for little or no reason."[16]

Life at the school revolved around survival rather than scholarship. And while shared suffering often forges community, the gentle, creative Jack found himself a social outcast among a small group of angry and rambunctious boys.

In his memoirs, Lewis would give Wynyard the nickname "Belsen," after a Nazi concentration camp. He suffered through two traumatizing years before the school was finally shut down and the sadistic headmaster was committed to an insane asylum.

From there, he enrolled in a string of boarding schools that were scarcely better than the first. He didn't come across any more barbaric headmasters, but neither did he find friends who understood him or teachers who engaged him.

For a young boy once cocooned by "endless books" and Warnie's company, the abrupt loss of both mental stimulation and brotherly love was too much to bear in the wake of his mother's death. "For many years, Joy (as I have defined it) was not only absent but forgotten," Lewis recalled.[17]

Despite the failings of his educational experiences to this point, Jack already had a sharp analytical mind. He surveyed the facts: His mother was gone. Her faith and his own prayers had failed to save her. The world was "a menacing and unfriendly place."[18]

With careful consideration, he reached his conclusion. Religion was "utterly false" and "a kind of endemic nonsense into which humanity tended to blunder."[19] He saw no reason to believe Christianity was an exception.

And so C.S. Lewis, "with no sense of loss but with the greatest relief," discarded the faith of his childhood.[20]

Despite Flora's hopes and prayers on her deathbed, the Bible she'd left for her youngest son had failed to reach him in the dark night of his adolescence. But another book soon would—setting Lewis on a trajectory that would shape his legacy forever.

CHAPTER 44

Stepping off a train at Great Bookham station in Surrey, a fifteen-year-old C.S. Lewis scanned the platform for W.T. Kirkpatrick. The man was easy to spot. Standing over six feet tall, he was lean but muscular and looked as if he'd come straight from digging around in the garden. He didn't draw attention from others at the station, but he was a legend in the Lewis household.

Lewis's father, Albert, and brother, Warnie, had both been tutored by Kirkpatrick and referred to him affectionately as the "Great Knock."[21] Lewis, however, eyed the sixty-six-year-old man with suspicion.

Walking over to introduce himself, Lewis stiffened with the dread any teenage boy feels at being wrapped in a hug by an old man who mistakes intimacy with one's parents as permission to act like old friends. But Kirkpatrick did nothing of the sort. He simply offered a firm handshake, turned on his heels, and headed for the door.

With some trepidation, Lewis fell into step beside him. After years of begging to be pulled from boarding school, his desperate letters to his father had finally gotten through. He was now to live with and study under the Great Knock. But despite the praise he'd heard all his life, he was filled with a sulky skepticism.

As they walked, Lewis looked around for a way to fill the increasingly awkward silence. Resorting to small talk, he commented that the "scenery" of Surrey was "wilder" than he'd expected.

"Stop!" demanded Kirkpatrick, giving Lewis a jolt of surprise. "What do you mean by wildness and what grounds had you for not expecting it?"

Lewis, having never been asked to defend such a casual remark, was nearly speechless. His stumbling response was met with a stinging series of follow-up questions, each more difficult to answer than the last.

"A few passes sufficed to show that I had no clear and distinct idea corresponding to the word 'wildness,' and that, in so far as I had any idea at all, 'wildness' was a singularly inept word," Lewis later recalled.

"Do you not see, then, that your remark was meaningless?" asked Kirkpatrick. "Do you not see, then, that you had no right to have any opinion whatever on the subject?"[22]

And so began Lewis's education under the Great Knock. The conversation was the first of countless to come. What may have crushed a boy of lesser mental aptitude was like "red beef and strong beer" to Lewis, who was overjoyed at finally being taught how to think rather than what to think.[23]

Over the next few years, he flourished under the challenge of learning new languages, debating philosophical questions, and translating classic literature. At the same time, still heady with the relief of discarding his family's Christianity, he was pleased to discover his new tutor was an atheist.

Lewis had walked his own path to atheism—which began with bitter anguish in his heart and culminated in a conscious decision of his mind—before arriving at Bookham. But studying under a brilliant atheist, he accrued new arguments to solidify his position. As he grew increasingly confident in his conclusions, he had no idea God was already mounting a response—one that would also begin in Lewis's heart long before it reached his mind.

It began on a Friday night in October. Lewis had spent a pleasant day in the nearby town of Leatherhead and was awaiting a train back to Bookham. The train platform was nearly empty as he paused to admire the deep blues and purples from a fading sunset. The temperature dropped, and Lewis felt a shiver—from both the crisp, cold air and the anticipation of the relaxing weekend that stretched out in front of him.

Why not get started now, he thought? Seeing his train pull into the station, Lewis quickly grabbed a book from the station bookstall and climbed aboard. That night, he began to read a story of tree spirits and fairy queens and the pursuit of beauty.

He was immediately spellbound.

"It is as if I were carried sleeping across the frontier, or as if I had died in the old country and could never remember how I came alive in the new," Lewis would later recall. To his great surprise, the "Joy blowing through" the novel didn't dissipate when he closed the cover but somehow continued to waft through the real world around him.[24]

It would be years before Lewis could describe what he'd experienced in the novel as a "bright shadow" of "holiness."[25] But the transcendent nature of the book was no accident.

The book was *Phantastes* and its author, George MacDonald, was a Christian and a former pastor. As one MacDonald biographer explains, the author "never saw [his novels] primarily as entertainment but as a way of communicating his vision of the immensity of God's love" and his kingdom.[26]

Recalling that train ride years later, Lewis would write, "That night my imagination was, in a certain sense, baptised; the rest of me, not unnaturally, took longer. I had not the faintest notion what I had let myself in for by buying *Phantastes*."[27]

Of course, *Phantastes* didn't preach the gospel explicitly. If it had, Lewis wouldn't have picked it up in the first place. Rather, its author sought "to evoke a sense of wonder in the reader, reminding us that there is more to the world than meets the eye."[28]

Lewis would eventually take a similar approach in *The Lion, the Witch and the Wardrobe*. He wouldn't write that book until his thirties, but even during his teen years with the Great Knock, God was planting seeds that would grow into the magical, snow-laden trees of the Narnian forest. *Phantastes* was only one of those seeds.

There was also the day that, running his fingers over an atlas of the classical world, Lewis would stop short at the name of an ancient Italian town. "Narnia," he read aloud slowly, and then again, louder, with a sense of wonder.

Then there was the day that a weeklong snowfall imbued the surrounding pines with a sense of magic, and Lewis imagined "a faun walking through the snow in the woods while carrying packages wrapped in brown paper and holding an umbrella."[29]

But seeds take a long time to grow into trees. And from his bed in Bookham, Lewis could hear the distant sounds of gunfire in France. The world was at war, and young men were dying on the front lines almost as quickly as they arrived.

England needed more bodies. Mr. Tumnus would have to wait.

CHAPTER 45

When C.S. Lewis first laid eyes on Oxford University's fabled spires, he was equally sure of two things: He wanted to be an Oxford scholar. And he wouldn't live long enough to do it.

His initial impressions were formed during a short visit for entry examinations in late 1916. "[Oxford] has surpassed my wildest dreams," he wrote to his father. "I never saw anything so beautiful, especially on these frosty moonlight nights."[30]

All his life, Lewis had heard his father bemoan the drudgery of work. "I had heard ever since I could remember, and believed, that adult life was to be an unremitting struggle in which the best I could hope for was to avoid the workhouse by extreme exertion," he recalled.[31]

But studying under the Great Knock and walking the picturesque grounds at Oxford didn't feel like misery. Lewis began to wonder if the work of an academic might bring about the joy he had been longing to recapture since childhood.

He enrolled as a student in the spring of 1917, but his first term held constant reminders that boys of his generation weren't growing up to become Oxford scholars—or anything else for that matter. They were dying on the front lines of World War I or right there in the halls of Oxford, half of which had been converted into hospitals for soldiers and officers.

Lewis was one of only seven undergraduates living on campus that term, and his own enlistment papers arrived just before finals. While waiting to hear where the British army would send him, he did two things common among young men facing imminent death on a battlefield.

First, he got "royally drunk."[32]

In doing so, he discovered the painful irony of heavy drinking: After reveling in the bliss of forgetting your greatest fears for a night, you often wake up with a whole new list of things you desperately hope no one else remembers.

In a letter to a friend, Lewis confessed to one dinner party where he drunkenly begged everyone present to let him whip them. Despite his offer to pay a shilling per lash, it doesn't seem anyone else was intoxicated enough to oblige him.

Lewis woke up in his room the next morning remembering nothing else but feeling a flush of shame.

His second action was a far more honorable one. He made a pact with a fellow soldier.

With every passing day in the dreadful war, more families got word that their sons and brothers had died on the battlefields. So Lewis and his roommate Paddy Moore made a solemn oath: If one died, the other would look after his family as if it were his own.

Lewis likely thought he was getting the better end of that deal. Paddy's father had abandoned the family, but Lewis found his friend's mother, Mrs. Janie Moore, to be attractive and engaging. She was also fairly young— the same age Flora had been when she'd died nine years prior.

The two hit it off immediately, and Lewis said he liked Mrs. Moore "immensely." As one biographer points out, "For the cynical, opinionated Jack Lewis, who rarely had a good word to say about anyone over the previous ten years, this was high praise indeed."[33]

At the same time, Lewis's relationship with his own father was a continued source of unmet expectations and mounting frustrations.

In letters home, Lewis attempted to grapple with fears of imminent death, but without fail, Albert's responses always steered the discussion back to practical matters. His father seemed just as unable or unwilling to help as he'd been following the loss of Flora. Finally convinced Albert would never truly listen to him, Lewis deemed any attempt at deeper conversation "a failure."[34]

Both men, unable to bridge the ever-widening emotional expanse between them, became unwilling to traverse any physical distance to connect either. When given a three-week leave from the army, Lewis chose to spend it with Paddy's family rather than his own.

And when Lewis sent a frantic telegram to let his father know he was being sent to the front lines, Albert feigned confusion at the message and failed to come see him off. The missed opportunity at what could have very well been a final goodbye was a deep cut for Lewis.

On November 29, 1917, C.S. Lewis was sent to the trenches at the front lines in France. It was his nineteenth birthday.

There is no such thing as a pleasant war, but World War I was particularly horrifying. For weeks on end and with no reprieve, young men slept, ate, hid, and fought in the "rancid mess of mixed mud and blood" of the frontline trenches. Ten million of them died in that squalor, their friends forced to carry on alongside their rotting bodies.[35]

Men who didn't lose their lives often lost their minds.

Many biographers have been puzzled to find that in his own memoirs, Lewis spent far more time bemoaning the horrors of boarding school than recounting the terrors of war. The difference was in the community he found at the front lines.

"Everyone you met took it for granted that the whole thing was an odious necessity, a ghastly interruption of rational life. And that made all the difference," wrote Lewis. "Straight tribulation…breeds camaraderie and even (when intense) a kind of love between the fellow-sufferers."

This stood in stark contrast to the "mutual distrust, cynicism, concealed and fretting resentment" he'd suffered through alone during his boarding school years.[36]

But if friendship was a balm to Lewis in his time as a soldier, it would prove to be a short-lived comfort. All his close friends from his first term at Oxford died in the conflict—including Paddy Moore.

In April 1918, Lewis himself was hit by shrapnel. With "the roar of exploding shells, the thud of impacting bullets, and the screams of wounded and dying men" ringing in his ears, an injured Lewis crawled through the mud, inch by inch, until a rescue party loaded him onto a stretcher and carried him away.[37]

Upon waking up in a hospital a day or two later, Lewis learned that the shrapnel lodged in his chest had come dangerously close to his heart. But that which almost killed him ultimately saved his life. His injuries, though not life-threatening, were just serious enough that he'd be sent back home to England.

After five months in the trenches, his time at the front lines was over. But his battles at home were just beginning.

CHAPTER 46

Scanning the open letter that lay on the table between him and his father, C.S. Lewis knew he'd been caught in a lie.

It was July 1919, and Lewis was visiting his father after delaying the trip for as long as he could. Every letter from home made him bristle these days, filled with Albert's probing questions about his son's finances. Again and again, Lewis waved his father off—he had fifteen pounds in his account, he said (equivalent to around 1,245 US dollars today). There was nothing for his father to worry about.

But just a day or two into Lewis's visit home, Albert had stumbled upon this opened letter from the bank. The truth was there in black and white: C.S. Lewis was overdrawn by twelve pounds. And Albert wanted an explanation.

The thick tension in the room wasn't because a meddling father had overstepped with his adult son. On the contrary, Albert's interest in the situation was justified. He was financially supporting Lewis, who was clearly spending money faster than Albert was sending it—and, to make matters worse, he was lying about it.

But when Lewis looked up at his father, it was hatred, not repentance, that was in his eyes. Ever since the day he'd been shipped off to the hell that was boarding school, Lewis's contempt for his father had been steadily building. No matter how guilty he might have felt, Lewis would not sit here now and be accused of lying by a man he no longer loved or respected.

And just like that, this confrontation was no longer about money. Over the next few minutes, Lewis shouted things he would regret for the rest of his life. With a sneer on his face and contempt in his voice, he unleashed a verbal tirade detailing each and every one of his father's failings since the day Flora died.

It's unclear what, if anything, Albert said in the moment, but he later recorded the incident in his journal. "[Jack] deceived me and said terrible, insulting, and despising things to me," he wrote.[38] The fight left him "miserable and heart sore."[39]

The argument and the visit came to an end. The tension between father and son did not.

Albert may have been emotionally obtuse, but he wasn't an idiot. He had growing suspicions that there was more going on with his son than a young adult forgetting to track his expenses.

In letters back and forth, Albert and Warnie exchanged notes about the youngest Lewis's behavior. They weren't entirely sure of the truth, but they were beginning to suspect he was caught in a web of lies—not just about how much he was spending but also about where he was going, what he was doing, and what exactly he was spending all that money on.

And they were almost certain that at the center of the web of lies lay a spider: Mrs. Janie Moore.

Upon his return from the front lines, Lewis had wasted no time in honoring his oath to his fallen friend Paddy. But very quickly, the relationship between Lewis and his friend's mother had surpassed the call of duty. It also surpassed the bounds of propriety.

To this day, biographers find Lewis's relationship with Mrs. Moore to be a source of mystery. On the surface, it appears innocent enough: a mother without her son and a son without his mother re-creating what they had lost with one another.

Mrs. Moore had also provided comfort and consistency when Lewis's only living parent failed to do so. When Lewis was sent to the front lines, it was she, not Albert, who'd been there to see him off. And when he was sent back to Europe to recover in a hospital, it was she, not Albert, who stayed by Lewis's bedside.

None of this behavior, on its own, would be particularly shocking, but the common conclusion among biographers is that Lewis had a sexual affair with his fallen friend's mom—and not just for one regrettable night but for years on end.

To be clear, there is no surviving proof, no damning letter with sordid details. But there is a suspicious mountain of lies: letters delivered in secret, clandestine vacations, and carefully orchestrated visits to hide the fact that they were living together. Something was going on that both Lewis and Mrs. Moore were eager to hide.

While much remains unclear about their relationship and likely always will, one thing is sure: Lewis saw Mrs. Moore and her teenage daughter as his new family.

With his big brother Warnie a world away, posted in China for military service, Lewis saw little need for his own biological family anymore—other than the checks he continued to cash from his father. After all, his new family had to live on something, and his own attempts at building a career weren't off to a very promising start.

His first choice, a fellowship at Oxford, didn't exist in the English department where he longed to work. His first published book, a work of poetry, was mostly ignored by both critics and the general public. And his first Oxford lecture, given while filling in for a philosophy teacher, had just four people in attendance.

Then, in the spring of 1925, Magdalen College at Oxford announced a new fellowship in English. Lewis rushed to apply. The next few weeks were marked by the particular anguish that always accompanies waiting to hear whether you've landed your dream job.

After a dizzying series of events that alternately raised and dashed his hopes, Lewis got the call. He was being elected to an official fellowship at Magdalen College as a tutor in English language and literature.

A few weeks later, he was inducted with all the pomp and circumstance a 467-year-old college can muster.

In a formal ceremony attended by his new colleagues, Lewis knelt before the president of Magdalen College, who read a passage in Latin. Then, the president beckoned Lewis to his feet, looked him in the eye, and declared, "I wish you *joy*."

Lewis proceeded around the room, stopping in front of each attendee in turn to hear them echo the refrain: "I wish you joy," "I wish you joy," "I wish you joy."

The significance of those words, spoken at that moment, was not lost on a man who'd been in the pursuit of joy all his life. An Oxford fellowship and the joy it would undoubtedly bring him were his at last.

Determined to make this five-year contract just the start of a long and happy career at Oxford, Lewis threw himself headlong into his work. Like many busy professionals with lofty career goals, he had little time for his estranged father. And then, before he knew it, time ran out.

On September 25, 1929, Albert Lewis died alone in a nursing home. Any chance for reconciliation died with him. Twenty-five years later, Lewis would confess, "I treated my own father abominably and no sin in my whole life now seems to be so serious."[40]

In bitterness and anger, Lewis had avoided his father right up to his dying day. But as he was about to discover, avoiding his heavenly Father would prove far more difficult.

CHAPTER 47

ewis was terrified.

Or, in his words, he was a fox "running in the open…bedraggled and weary, hounds barely a field behind." He was a mouse in the shadow of a cat. He was a man being outmaneuvered in a game of chess. He was a prodigal son being dragged home "kicking, struggling, resentful, and darting his eyes in every direction for a chance of escape."[41]

Lewis could feel a holy God—one he didn't believe in—closing in on him, and he had no shortage of metaphors to describe his horror.

It had started so simply: a cozy read on a Friday night. In *Phantastes*, Lewis had seen a "bright shadow coming out of the book into the real world and resting there, transforming all common things and yet itself unchanged."[42]

The story by George MacDonald had stirred Lewis's heart for something more, but his mind remained firm in its convictions. "It was a pity [Mac-Donald] had that bee in his bonnet about Christianity," he thought. "He was good in spite of it."[43]

But over the following years, Lewis, a voracious reader, began to observe a disturbing trend. His favorite novels, time and time again, were written by Christian writers and philosophers, while books by atheist writers (with whom he agreed wholeheartedly) "all seemed a little thin."[44]

By 1930, a thirty-one-year-old Lewis was seeing evidence of the existence of God everywhere he looked—ancient philosophy, contemporary literature, and even the lives of those around him. As someone who "had always wanted, above all things, not to be 'interfered with,'" Lewis chafed at the idea that his soul may not be solely his own.[45]

But he had to admit, fear of reality does not make that reality any less true. Lewis was alone in his room at Magdalen College when he conceded the point: "I gave in, and admitted that God was God, and knelt and prayed: perhaps, that night, the most dejected and reluctant convert in all England."[46]

He'd been cornered by the cat, outsmarted by his Adversary. And there was no joy in it at all.

Of course, conceding the existence of a God is not the same as declaring Jesus as King. Lewis remained convinced that Christianity's unique claims—of a man who was God walking the earth he created, dying for the sins of humanity, and defeating death—were nothing more than a myth.

Then he talked to Tolkien.

Today, J.R.R. Tolkien is best known as the author of arguably the most popular and critically acclaimed work of the twentieth century, *The Lord of the Rings*. But before Bilbo Baggins ever embarked on his first adventure, Tolkien was a mere Christian working as an English professor at Magdalen College.

As colleagues-turned-friends, Lewis and Tolkien could often be found quibbling over the minutiae of curricula one day and bonding over shared interests the next.

Their conversation on Saturday, September 19, 1931, started, like so many others, over a dinner followed by an evening stroll. As an early autumn breeze stirred the leaves overhead, the men turned to the topic of metaphor, myth, and Christianity. When dusk faded to darkness, the men returned to Lewis's room to continue the discussion.

Christianity *is* a myth, Tolkien agreed, in the sense that myths "capture the echoes of deeper truths." "Christianity tells a true story about humanity," Tolkien argued, "which makes sense of all the stories that humanity tells about itself."[47]

The conversation finally came to a close at 3:00 in the morning, but its effects on Lewis had just begun. Over the next nine days, he replayed the discussion again and again. And then, quite mysteriously, that immeasurable distance between heart and mind was closed in an instant.

Considering he'd go on to pen defining works of Christian apologetics, Lewis's description of his own conversion is maddeningly brief: "I was driven to Whipsnade (Zoo) one sunny morning. When we set out, I did not believe that Jesus Christ is the Son of God, and when we reached the zoo, I did."

The experience, he wrote, was "like when a man, after long sleep, still lying motionless in bed, becomes aware that he is now awake."[48]

We don't know much else about that trip to the zoo. Perhaps he paused to consider the lions, their quiet, majestic power an echo of the one true King—an echo waiting to be unleashed across a Narnian forest. Perhaps not.

But we do know this: In coming to Christ, Lewis did not feel the terror or reluctance that accompanied his conversion to theism. Instead, he felt a new clarity. He saw the seeds of joy planted by his mother, Warnie's toy garden, *Phantastes*, and his career for what they were: signposts pointing him to the Source of all true joy.

Now that he'd found it, it was Lewis's turn to erect new signposts for others "lost in the woods."[49] But he wouldn't change jobs or enter seminary to do it. He'd simply do what he'd always done. He'd pick up his pen and write.

CHAPTER 48

As smoke from his pipe filled the air above his head, Lewis peered around the room and waited. Half a dozen men were gathered together on a Thursday night, and he had just asked if anyone had brought something to read.

After waiting a beat, J.R.R. Tolkien, known as Tollers among friends, cleared his throat and reached down to pull out a stack of papers. As he began to read aloud his draft of *The Lord of the Rings*, Hugo Dyson grew restless. "Oh God, not another elf!" he protested.[50] But Lewis waved Dyson off. "Shut up, Hugo! Come on, Tollers!" he shouted, leaning in to hear what Tolkien was trying to say.[51]

This was a meeting of the Inklings, a group of Christian academics and writers who gathered regularly throughout the 1930s and 1940s to smoke pipes, drink tea or beer, and discuss their faith and work.

With regular feedback (and more than a little good-natured ribbing) from one another, members of the group produced some of the most critically acclaimed and best-selling works of their generation.

"The unpayable debt that I owe to [Lewis] was not 'influence' as it is ordinarily understood, but sheer encouragement," said Tolkien. "But for his interest and unceasing eagerness for more I should never have brought [*The Lord of the Rings*] to a conclusion."[52]

After publishing a few lesser-known works throughout the 1930s, Lewis released *The Problem of Pain*, a philosophical exploration of evil and suffering, in 1940. This was the book that caught the eye of a commissioning editor at the BBC, who then invited Lewis to give the wartime broadcasts of 1941–1942.

Those broadcasts catapulted Lewis into fame across Great Britain. And in 1942, the international release of *The Screwtape Letters* made him famous the world over.

There are two things that are always true of fame. The first, of course, is that it attracts a lot of attention.

As Lewis's star began to rise, he was flooded with letters, phone calls, and care packages from around the world. His brother, Warnie, answered around twelve thousand letters on his behalf, pecking out responses "with two fingers on his battered Royal typewriter."[53] When particularly relentless fans or journalists called the family home demanding to speak to C.S. Lewis personally, Warnie would "lift the receiver and say 'Oxford Sewage Disposal Unit,' and go on repeating it until they went away."[54]

The care packages—often sent by wealthy Americans enjoying a postwar prosperity that had yet to reach England—were much more welcomed by the Lewis household. They typically included food and stationery. One fan sent a tuxedo. Another sent a ham. (The Inklings so enjoyed that one that the sender, an American named Dr. Warfield Firor, sent several more, earning him the nickname "Firor-of-the-Hams" and a thank-you letter signed by everyone in the group.)

Lewis also garnered attention from the press, even appearing on the cover of *Time* magazine in 1947, though some articles were more accurate than others. As one biographer recounts, "Tolkien was particularly amused by one media reference to an 'Ascetic Mr. Lewis.' This bore no relation to the Lewis he knew. That very morning, Tolkien had told his son that Lewis had 'put away three pints in a very short session.'"[55]

The second reality of fame is that fans never really know what life is like for the person in the spotlight. Not even Lewis's closest friends knew the incredible pressure he was facing at home.

After World War II came to a close, life only got harder for the now-famous author. Warnie had returned from active service and spiraled into alcoholism. His frequent binges were a heavy burden for a younger brother to bear, especially in a time when alcoholism was treated as a shameful family secret.

And then there was Mrs. Moore. Long gone were the happy, if perhaps scandalous, early days of their relationship. Even before she developed dementia, Mrs. Moore was "increasingly irritable and confused," interrupting Lewis's work every ten minutes with new demands, real or invented.[56]

And yet, Lewis never complained. He never wavered from his promise to his friend, faithfully caring for Paddy Moore's mother for thirty years.

It was only after Mrs. Moore's death in 1951 that he finally lamented, "I have lived most of it (my private life) in a house which was hardly ever at peace for 24 hours among senseless wranglings, lyings, back bitings, follies and scares. I never went home without a feeling of terror as to what appalling situation might have developed in my absence."[57]

Life at work held even more challenges for Lewis, whose popularity with the general public made him the scorn of some Oxford academics. The men who had once "wished him joy" now passed over Lewis three times for positions he wanted and for which he was well qualified. As friends and colleagues celebrated promotions—including Tolkien, who was made a professor at age thirty-one—Lewis remained lower on the totem pole as a fellow and a tutor.

Even the Inklings let Lewis down eventually. After years of dwindling attendance at their Thursday meetings, the group's gatherings came to an unceremonious end on October 27, 1949. Lewis prepared to host his friends as usual. He brewed some tea, had tobacco at the ready. But nobody came.

Lewis once advised a friend, "Whenever you are fed up with life, start writing: ink is the great cure for all human ills, as I have found out long ago."[58] And so, taking his own advice, he decided to write his way out of his trials.

But this time, he wanted to write something different from the scholarly and theological works that had made him famous. He wanted to write a book for children—a book that might engage their imaginations as *Phantastes* had once engaged his.

When Lewis first shared the idea with a couple of close friends, they laughed at him. What could an unmarried, childless professor like him possibly know about children? But Lewis couldn't shake the mental picture he'd had back in Bookham of a faun walking in a snowy wood. And the face of a lion kept dominating his dreams.

"At first I had very little idea how the story [of *The Lion, the Witch and the Wardrobe*] would go," Lewis later recalled. "But then suddenly Aslan came bounding into it...[O]nce He was there He pulled the whole story together, and soon He pulled the six other Narnian stories in after Him."[59]

From 1950 to 1956, Lewis published all seven books from the Narnia series in rapid succession. His fan base continued to grow. But one admirer across the Atlantic Ocean wanted to be more than pen pals with her favorite author.

Clutching a few treasured letters Lewis had written in response to her own, Joy Davidman boarded a ship and set sail for England with one goal in her mind: She was going to seduce C.S. Lewis.

CHAPTER 49

C.S. Lewis wasn't looking for a wife.

He'd befriended plenty of women, especially those who were poets or authors. But after appeasing Mrs. Moore for most of his life, fifty-three-year-old Lewis had no interest in bringing another woman into his home.

Nothing about his initial meeting with Joy Davidman, over lunch in a hotel lobby in Oxford, changed any of that. Before they met in person, the two had exchanged a few letters. In them, Lewis had learned that Joy was an American, a wife, and the mother of two boys. She was intelligent and widely read. And like him, she'd moved from atheism to Christianity in adulthood.

When a letter arrived in which Joy announced that she was coming to England, Lewis didn't hesitate to accept her invitation to lunch, where she proved to be a sharp conversationalist and pleasant company. As their meal came to a close, he politely invited her to dine with him again if she could find the time before she returned to America.

He had no idea she'd purchased only a one-way ticket—or that she wanted far more from Lewis than a second lunch.

Lewis's writings—first his published books and then the letters he sent in response to hers—had become a lifeline for Joy. She grew desperate to meet this man whose kind demeanor, generous spirit, and rational mind stood in stark contrast to her own unfaithful, volatile, and frequently drunk husband. As one biographer puts it, "While others merely sought Lewis's advice, Davidman sought his soul."[60]

Joy accepted Lewis's invitation to a second lunch—and a few more after that—before her plans were cut short by a letter from her husband. He wrote to say he had fallen in love with her cousin who, escaping a violent marriage of her own, had moved in with him and cared for Joy's young sons while she was away.

Joy was forced to return to America in January 1953, but after finalizing her divorce, she sailed back to England in November with her eight- and nine-year-old sons in tow. She did not, however, come with a work visa.

With no way to generate income for herself, Joy fell on Lewis's generosity. He arranged for a lease and paid the rent on a three-bedroom house for her and her boys.

Joy's own son could see that her intention was "to seduce C.S. Lewis."[61] But she was sixteen years his junior, and Lewis saw her as only a friend, albeit a treasured one. In Joy, Lewis found an editor, collaborator, sounding board, and encourager. She provided valuable feedback on his work, especially the book *Till We Have Faces*, which he dedicated to her.

Then, in 1956, Joy's visa ran out. As a formerly public member of the Communist Party, Joy was afraid to return to America during the height of McCarthy's Red Scare. So she went to Lewis for help once again.

Unwilling to lose his literary muse and friend, Lewis agreed to marry Joy in a civil ceremony to prevent her deportation. Warnie was appalled, but Lewis insisted it was an "innocent little secret," a legal formality and nothing more.[62] The two brothers could continue living out their days together as bachelors.

But three things happened in rapid succession that would change the Lewis household forever.

First, Joy insisted on moving in with her new husband, bringing her boys with her. As his wife, she knew she had not secured Lewis's heart, but as she saw it, she still had rights to his home. Much to Warnie's chagrin, Lewis relented.

Second, the closer proximity allowed both Lewis men to get to know Joy better. She was quick-witted and could hold her own with even their most educated friends. Lewis grew to enjoy her company more and more, often staying up late to discuss literature or challenge her in Scrabble. (The two played according to their own more advanced set of rules. Any word from any language, real or invented, that had ever appeared in a book was fair game.)

And third, Joy got very, very sick. When a simple fall led to a broken femur, X-rays revealed a malignant tumor in her breast. The cancer was already spreading. She was dying.

Suddenly faced with the reality of losing Joy, Lewis was also forced to face a truth that had somewhat snuck up on him. He was, he now saw, in love with Joy.

On March 21, 1957, he married her again—this time in a bedside ceremony in the hospital, and this time as a true union before God.

Doctors expected Joy to pass within a few days, but God granted the newlyweds a miracle. She began to recover. Pretty soon, she was able to get out of bed and return home. The following summer, the couple even embarked on a ten-day belated honeymoon in Ireland, marking Lewis's first time on an airplane, which he found "enchanting."[63]

Lewis had two years to love and care for his wife, which he did even as osteoporosis wreaked havoc on his own body. Then, on July 13, 1960, with her loving husband by her bedside, Joy succumbed to cancer and stepped into eternity.

Lewis was distraught.

Twenty years prior, he had contemplated the philosophical implications of pain, death, and loss in his book *The Problem of Pain*, which led to his discovery and fame. But now, he was forced to live it personally.

When Joy's "death unleashed a stream of thoughts which Lewis could not initially control," he wrote them down as a way of coping, resulting in "one of his most distressing and disturbing books: *A Grief Observed*."[64]

In his grief, he lamented the ways in which photographs of his beloved wife, and even his own memories of her, paled in comparison to the real thing. But that unmet longing once again pointed Lewis back to "the source from which those arrows of Joy had been shot at [him] ever since childhood."[65]

"I need Christ, not something that resembles Him," he wrote.[66]

In love and loss, Lewis recognized that only joy rooted in Christ and his kingdom is eternal. He'd buried his parents, his fellow soldiers, and now his bride. Life, he understood, is "a mist that appears for a little time and then vanishes" (James 4:14, ESV).

Or in the words of Shakespeare's King Lear, "Men must endure their going hence." Those words, already etched on his mother's tombstone, would soon be engraved on his.[67]

CHAPTER 50

On November 22, 1963, a world leader and a college professor each prepared for an ordinary day. President John F. Kennedy looked over his notes for a speech he'd give in Fort Worth, soon to leave for Dallas in an open motorcade. C.S. Lewis had breakfast, answered letters, and solved a crossword.

By the end of the day, they'd both be gone.

It was just after lunchtime when Warnie noticed that his brother seemed tired. He suggested Lewis take a nap. But at 5:30, a loud crash came from the bedroom. Warnie rushed in "to find Lewis collapsed, unconscious, at the foot of the bed." After several years of declining health, C.S. Lewis had died of "renal failure, prostate obstruction, and cardiac degeneration."[68]

Just one hour later, shots rang out in downtown Dallas, Texas. Lee Harvey Oswald took aim at Kennedy from an open window in a nearby building and struck his target.

Lewis and Kennedy, as it turns out, had much more in common than the date on their death certificates. Both men were Irish. Both went by the nickname Jack. Both were veterans of a world war. And both gained global renown through their writing and speaking.

There was one key difference in their fame, however. Kennedy worked to build his own image and secure his own legacy—a legacy his widow compared to King Arthur's kingdom of Camelot.

Lewis, on the other hand, lived and worked for the kingdom of God. As he put it, "All that is not eternal is eternally out of date."[69]

He had no visions of lasting notoriety, despite the attention his work had garnered in his lifetime. According to one biographer, Lewis told a friend "that he expected to be forgotten within five years of his death."[70] He was at peace with that likely outcome.

And in the days immediately following their deaths, it seemed likely that only one man's legacy would live on.

Kennedy's death dominated the front page of every major newspaper on earth. In most papers, Lewis's death wasn't even mentioned. While more than eight hundred thousand people lined the streets to watch Kennedy's funeral procession, there was no procession at all for Lewis, his funeral attended by only a handful of close friends. His grief-stricken brother, spiraling into another alcoholic binge, couldn't even get out of bed for the memorial and didn't bother to invite anyone else.

But in the decades since that fateful day, the impact of Kennedy's Camelot has faded while Lewis's influence has only grown.

In 2013, the *New York Times* called Lewis an "Evangelical Rock Star," while *Time* magazine named him the "hottest theologian" of the year—forty-two years after his death. Comparing the legacies of Kennedy and Lewis, a journalist for the *Atlantic* was forced to admit that "Lewis's ideas claim the most lasting influence, both on the Christian tradition and on the Western culture beyond."[71]

In 2000, *Christianity Today* asked more than a hundred "church leaders" to nominate the ten best religious books of the twentieth century. According to the magazine, "By far, C.S. Lewis was the most popular author and *Mere Christianity* the book nominated most often. Indeed, we could have included even more Lewis works, but finally we had to say: 'Enough is enough; give some other authors a chance.'"[72]

Despite Lewis's expectation that he would die and be forgotten, he "has made the most difficult transition an author can hope to make—being read by more people a generation after his death than before it."[73]

His work has endured for decades. And yet a close look at his life makes it clear that Lewis served not the work itself but rather the God who gave him that work.

Instead of competing with others, he supported and celebrated the accomplishments of fellow authors, even nominating Tolkien for the Nobel Prize in Literature in 1961. Instead of building wealth, he lived so generously that he was often unsure whether he'd be able to pay his own bills. And instead of using the demands of his work as an excuse to isolate himself from the needs of those around him, he loved and served others selflessly.

In life, Lewis lived for the glory of God and the good of others. And in death, he beheld the full expression of that which had proved so fleeting on earth: joy.

We are all, he wrote in a letter to a friend, like "a seed patiently waiting in the earth: waiting to come up a flower in the Gardener's good time, up into the real world, the real waking."[74]

By the time his own "real waking" arrived that November day, Lewis had lived a full life. Through story and reason, he'd learned to love the Lord his God with all his heart, all his soul, and all his mind. Then he'd set out to help others do the same—not as a pastor with a pulpit but as a professor with a pen.

On November 22, 1963, he scribbled out a few letters to friends and then laid that pen down for the last time. But when he stepped into eternity, he discovered the truth: The impact of his life and work had only just begun.

I (Jordan) know tons of people who love C.S. Lewis's stories but very few who know *his* story. That's a shame because, as you've now seen, Lewis's story is an *incredible* one. It's not only dramatic and entertaining but also profoundly helpful. The author of *Mere Christianity* has helped me—a mere Christian like Lewis himself—understand what it looks like to change the world from the pew rather than the pulpit. I hope you can say the same. But just to be sure, here are a few ways that you and I can follow Lewis's lead and glorify God through our work today.

I. MERE CHRISTIANS GLORIFY GOD BY FINDING THEIR ULTIMATE JOY IN CHRIST, NOT THEIR WORK.

Work was God's first gift to humankind (see Genesis 1:26-28). And like any good earthly father, our heavenly Father undoubtedly delights in watching his children enjoy the gift he gave us. Ecclesiastes 2:24 says this explicitly: "A person can do nothing better than to eat and drink and find satisfaction in their own toil. This too, I see, is from the hand of God."

I hope everything in this book has convinced you that we *should* find joy in our work. But we should never expect to find *ultimate* joy in our work, spouse, children, travel experiences, or any other created thing. Why? Because God says it's impossible. Jesus said, "Remain in my love...I have told you this so that my joy may be in you and that your joy may be complete" (John 15:9, 11). In other words, you and I will never find "complete" joy apart from Christ.

Like so many of us, C.S. Lewis learned this the hard way. As a boy, Lewis tasted joy for the first time in the form of a cookie tin garden created by his brother Warnie. But after the loss of his mother, all joy seemed to dissipate for Lewis. He spent the next couple of decades trying to rekindle it through alcohol, an illicit affair, and, of course, his work.

Undoubtedly, Lewis found some momentary happiness in these pursuits. When he was inducted as a fellow at Magdalen College and his colleagues looked him in the eye to wish him "joy," I guarantee that Lewis believed he had finally found it in full. After all, he had achieved his vocational dream!

But by God's grace, Lewis came to learn what every successful professional inevitably does: that no amount of achievement is ever enough. Without Christ, even a dream job will eventually turn into a nightmare. Here's how Lewis himself said it years later:

> God designed the human machine to run on Himself. He Himself is the fuel our spirits were designed to burn, or the food our spirits were designed to feed on. There is no other. That is why it is just no good asking God to make us happy in our own way without bothering about religion. God cannot give us a happiness and peace apart from Himself, because it is not there. There is no such thing.[75]

Is your mood perfectly correlated to whether you're winning at work? Do you spend less time with the Lord when things aren't going your way? Are you unable to enjoy God's gift of rest from your work?

Take it from someone with *loads* of experience in this area: If you answered yes to any of those questions, you're probably looking to your work to provide you with the ultimate joy that can be found only in Christ.

If that's you, let me encourage you to do three things right now.

First, *confess your idolatry to God and other mere Christians.* Sunshine is the best disinfectant. So long as you keep your idolatry in the dark, it's going to be nearly impossible to battle against it.

Second, *meditate on the gospel.* You and I were once God's enemies. Now we are adopted children of God (see 1 John 3:1-3). You will never earn a loftier title or accolade than that. Meditating on that truth daily is what will free you to pursue professional accolades not to find ultimate joy but in response to it.

Finally, *ask the Lord for his power* to enjoy the good gift of work without turning it into an idolatrous ultimate good and the source of your self-worth. In doing this, you will be glorifying God as you work!

2. MERE CHRISTIANS GLORIFY GOD BY EVANGELIZING WITH THEIR WORK AND NOT JUST THEIR WORDS.

Our definition of *evangelism* tends to be *really* narrow—essentially, talking through the "Romans Road" with a nonbeliever.

But God's definition is much broader. Psalm 19 says that "the heavens declare the glory of God," even though the stars "use no words."

It's not just stars that evangelize without words though. All throughout Scripture, we see humans evangelizing and bringing glory to God simply by how they worked. Take Nehemiah as just one example. After rebuilding the walls of Jerusalem in an astonishingly fast fifty-two days, Nehemiah's enemies were forced to give God credit and glory because they "realized that this work had been done with the help of our God" (Nehemiah 6:16).

These passages point to an important truth: You don't have to be evangelizing with your words to glorify God. You can also glorify him by evangelizing with your work. In what you do—the *products* of your work—and how you do it—the *processes* by which you work—you can create cravings in non-Christians for things that are true, noble, right, pure, lovely, admirable, excellent, and praiseworthy (see Philippians 4:8).

And the creation of those cravings is good in and of itself. Why? Because if the craving you're creating through your work can only be satisfied in full in Christ, you are setting non-Christians down a path that dead ends at a single true Source.

The life of C.S. Lewis is exhibit A for how this happens. It wasn't the words of a sermon that caused Lewis to doubt his atheism but an exceptional work of fiction. In *Phantastes*, a seemingly "secular" novel about tree spirits and fairy queens, Lewis saw glimpses of joy, love, and beauty that caused a *craving* in his heart for more. That longing sent Lewis down a long and winding path in search of truth. And his craving was fully satisfied only when he met Christ as his personal Lord and Savior.

Later, Lewis followed the same playbook in his own novels, most notably *The Chronicles of Narnia*. He didn't conclude *The Lion, the Witch and the*

Wardrobe with an epilogue spelling out the parallels between Aslan and Christ. Lewis was content to baptize the imagination of his readers, leaving them with a craving for a world of wonder, adventure, and sacrificial love that could only be fully satisfied by the "true myth" of Christianity.[76]

Your work can evangelize in much the same way, believer. *Everything* you do at work testifies to the God you believe in—not just the words you speak. So here's my question for you: *What about the product or process of your work is creating a craving in others that will only be fully satisfied in Christ?*

Maybe you're an artist like Lewis, and for you, it's the stories of sacrificial love you tell in your production of songs, films, or novels. Maybe you're a mechanic, and it's the process by which you work with joy that seems other-worldly to non-Christians. Maybe you're an entrepreneur, and it's the product of a workplace culture that values people more than their productivity.

I know I've just dropped a big question in your lap, but I'd encourage you not to skip over it. Dedicate fifteen minutes to sit with it and really unpack how you can evangelize with your work and not just your words, all to God's greater glory.

3. MERE CHRISTIANS GLORIFY GOD BY EMBRACING THEIR UNIQUE POSITION TO MAKE DISCIPLES OF JESUS CHRIST.

I grew up in a church culture that assumed the best way to "make disciples of all nations" (Matthew 28:19) was for Christians to leave their location and vocation to serve as "full-time missionaries" overseas.

But history tells a *very* different story.

According to pastor Tim Keller's research, "80% or more of evangelism in the early church" when Christianity *exploded* around the world "was done not by ministers or evangelists" but by tentmakers, shepherds, and merchants.[77] It has *always* been mere Christians who have done the most for the "Great Commission." And experts argue that will continue to be true for at least the next hundred years.[78]

Why? Because the fastest-growing religious affiliation in the West is *no* religious affiliation.[79] Non-Christians are less likely than ever to step inside a church to learn about Jesus for the first time. So where will they hear the good news? *Through you and me* working alongside them Monday through Friday.

You and I have a level of access to non-Christians that donor-supported missionaries only *dream* of. We also tend to have stories that are more relatable to the lost.

See C.S. Lewis as a case in point. On paper, it made no sense that the BBC would choose a literature professor from Oxford to deliver their wartime religious broadcasts. But as Lewis explained, the BBC chose him to be the voice of Christianity to the British people *precisely because he was not* a religious professional. He "had a past" he wasn't proud of and a "real job" the average person could understand and relate to. And it was because of those things that he was welcomed as a friend by Brits across religious lines.

Lewis understood that, as a mere Christian, he had a uniquely powerful position to make disciples of Jesus Christ. But he glorified God not just by *knowing* that as intellectual fact but by *embracing* his unique position to boldly proclaim the gospel.

You and I are called to do the same today. Yes, there are times in which we are only called to evangelize wordlessly with our work. But there are other times in which we are also called to speak up on behalf of our King.

The question is how? What does it look like practically to make disciples in our increasingly post-Christian context? Here are three answers to that question.

First, *pray for the salvation of specific people you work with*. Right now, write down the names of five lost coworkers, customers, or vendors. And pray "that God may open a door for our message, so that we may proclaim the mystery of Christ" (Colossians 4:3).

Second, *be so good they can't ignore you*. Lewis would have never been tapped by the BBC had he not been exceptional at his craft of writing and teaching. Similarly, it is likely to be your excellence at work that will "win the respect of outsiders" (1 Thessalonians 4:11-12) and make them eager to listen to anything you have to say.

Finally, *look for opportunities to move conversations from the surface to the serious to the spiritual*. We don't have to wait for a non-Christian to "ask the question" about what makes us different. With a bit of intentionality, it's easy to steer conversations with the lost from surface-level things (How's your marathon training going?) to serious things (Why do you love running so much?) and then to spiritual things (Would you describe running as a religious experience for you?).

This method works for me and other mere Christians I know who are great at making disciples at work. Whatever works for you works. But don't fall for the enemy's lie that the Great Commission is only or even primarily for the missionaries pictured on your refrigerator. Every follower of Jesus is called to make disciples. And as a mere Christian, you are in an *ideal* position to do so today!

There's a day coming soon when you'll meet Fred Rogers, Fannie Lou Hamer, Ole Kirk Christiansen, Hannah More, and C.S. Lewis in the resurrected flesh. Sitting around a campfire on an idyllic night on the New Earth, you'll get to hear their stories firsthand.

Now, Satan would love you to believe two things as you envision this scene.

First, *you can't have as great of an impact as these heroes in your own work today.* That's a lie. I (Jordan) have said it a couple of times in this book, but it's worth emphasizing once more: The same Holy Spirit that empowered these five men and women now works through you and me.

It is not just you going to work tomorrow but "God who works in you to will and to act in order to fulfill his good purpose" (Philippians 2:13). And "the Spirit God gave us does not make us timid, but gives us power, love and self-discipline" (2 Timothy 1:7) to do "immeasurably more than all we ask or imagine" for God's glory and the good of others (Ephesians 3:20).

Here's the second thing Satan would love you to believe: *If you don't have as great of an impact as the heroes in this book, your story isn't worth telling.* Nope. That's another lie from "the father of lies" (John 8:44).

It's not just the stories of people told in books like this one that God promises to remember. Hebrews 6:10 promises that God "will not forget *your* work," or the stories of any one of his chosen people.

And let's not forget that the people whose stories are told in *the* Book are rarely the rich and famous. Instead, Scripture is filled with tales of mere Christians like you and me: tentmakers like Paul, Priscilla, and Aquila; tax collectors like Zacchaeus; and entrepreneurs like Mary, Joanna, and Susanna who funded Jesus's ministry. It wasn't job titles and accolades that made these believers' stories worth telling but rather their faithfulness to "Jesus, the author and perfecter of [their] faith" (Hebrews 12:2, NASB).

Now that we've silenced Satan's lies, let's go back to imagining that campfire scene together. Just as the last of these five mere Christians finishes telling you their story, you sense Someone approaching. You look up and can't believe your eyes. It's the Alpha and the Omega. The Lion of Judah. Jesus the King. And he wants to know if the seat beside you is taken.

Everyone stands at the sound of his voice. But Jesus insists that we all keep our seats. He has come to hear *your* story. He knows every detail of it, of course. But he wants Fred Rogers, Fannie Lou Hamer, Ole Kirk Christiansen, Hannah More, C.S. Lewis, and all who are gathered around to hear it too.

So here's my question for you as we close this book: *What stories will you tell on that day that will give Christ greater glory?* What is it about how you are stewarding your sacred work today that will lead to spontaneous shouts of praise around that eternal campfire?

I pray this book has baptized your imagination to that end and given you concrete answers to that question. I hope it has given you five heroes to carry with you as three-dimensional models of what it looks like practically to follow Christ in your vocation. And I pray this book has set you on a path to glorifying God more fully in your good and sacred work.

A FREE BOOK AND OTHER RESOURCES

A FREE COPY FOR YOUR MERE CHRISTIAN FRIENDS

Most of your Christian friends are *not* serving God as pastors or donor-supported missionaries. They are serving faithfully as mere Christians, working as small business owners, artists, Uber drivers, teachers, and retail employees. And they, like you, *deeply* desire to glorify God in their work.

I (Jordan) want to help you help your friends to that end by giving them a free copy of part 1 of this book on the faith and work of Fred Rogers. Send it to your friends now at JordanRaynor.com/free.

Your friends will get a great e-book. And you will have some shared language to discuss how you can glorify God as mere Christians today. It's my way of saying thank you for reading this book!

WHAT SHOULD YOU READ NEXT?

Thank you for reading *Five Mere Christians*!

If you loved this book, you will likely enjoy the weekly devotional I (Jordan) write for mere Christians called "The Word Before Work," which you can subscribe to for free at JordanRaynor.com/devotionals.

Want to go deeper than those short devotionals? Check out my bestselling books that go deeper on some of the themes we explored in *Five Mere Christians*.

The Sacredness of Secular Work: 4 Ways Your Job Matters for Eternity (Even When You're Not Sharing the Gospel)

Redeeming Your Time: 7 Biblical Principles for Being Purposeful, Present, and Wildly Productive

Master of One: Find and Focus on the Work You Were Created to Do

Called to Create: A Biblical Invitation to Create, Innovate, and Risk

WANT TO HEAR STORIES OF MODERN MERE CHRISTIANS LIKE YOU?

Then check out the *Mere Christians* podcast! Each week, I (Jordan) interview guests across the widest variety of vocations about how they seek to glorify God through their seemingly "secular" work. Here are some of my past guests:

- Anne Beiler (founder of Auntie Anne's)
- Jodi Benson (voice of Ariel in *The Little Mermaid*)
- Candace Cameron Bure (actress)
- Tamika Catchings (four-time Olympic gold medalist)
- Dr. Francis Collins (former director of the National Institutes of Health)
- Tony Dungy (NFL Hall of Fame coach)
- Joni Eareckson Tada (painter)
- Scott Harrison (founder of charity: water)
- Horst Schulze (cofounder of the Ritz Carlton)
- Aarti Sequeira (Food Network host)

Subscribe for free on Apple Podcasts, Spotify, or JordanRaynor.com/podcast.

WHICH MERE CHRISTIANS DO YOU WANT TO SEE IN VOLUME 2?

Kaleigh and I (Jordan) have a long list of mere Christians whose stories we are considering telling in a second volume of this book. Vote for the five stories *you* want to hear most at JordanRaynor.com/mc2.

ACKNOWLEDGMENTS

JORDAN'S ACKNOWLEDGMENTS

To my cowriter, Kaleigh Cox: I am rarely at a loss for words, but I am having a *supremely* difficult time communicating how grateful I am for you. I knew that working with a cowriter for the first time was an *incredibly* risky prospect. But big risks lead to bigger rewards—see this book as a case in point. I've hired dozens of people throughout my career, and I can count on one hand the number of people who have far exceeded my expectations. You are one of them. If I get any more credit for this book than you, it will be a great injustice; you have been a true partner in this project. Thank you for allowing God to use you and your extraordinary gifts in this way. I'm praying we get to write *many* more volumes of this book together!

To my fellow mere Christians, especially the members of the Mere Christians Community: Thank you for constantly showing me what it looks like to glorify God in work outside the four walls of the church. Many of your stories will be in a book like this someday. Many others will be told around New Earth campfires for billions of years, all to Christ's greater glory.

To my bride, Kara: Thank you for listening to me excitedly share these stories with you first. And thank you for putting up with my "unhealthy obsession" (your words) with Fred Rogers.

To my daughters, Ellison, Kate, and Emery: Thank you for the killer idea for the conclusion of this book! I'm always on the lookout for heroes for you three. The five women and men in this book are some of the best I know of. Follow them as they followed Christ.

To my longtime assistant, Kayla: You are one of the great blessings of my life. Thank you for your terrific work as usual on this book—and for spending *way* too much time with Florence Nightingale only to leave her on the threshing floor.

To my agent, D.J. Snell: We knew selling this book was going to be an uphill battle, but you did it. Thank you for getting this important book made! Let's make a lot more...

To Kyle Hatfield, Barb Sherrill, Brad Moses, Heather Green, Bob Hawkins, Heidi Picinic, Naomi Burns, and the entire team at Harvest House: You all caught the vision for this book when few other publishers did. Thank you for taking a risk on this innovative concept!

To the Author and perfecter of my faith: I am still amazed at the miracle of my salvation. Thank you for saving me not just *from* something but *for* something: partnering with you in the good works you prepared in advance for me and other mere Christians to do. *Soli Deo gloria.*

KALEIGH'S ACKNOWLEDGMENTS

To Jordan Raynor: Thank you for taking a chance on an unknown mere Christian like me. I've been thankful for your work since I first discovered it in 2017, and now I'm thankful for your friendship too.

To Ashlee Gadd and Andrew Peterson: Thank you for *Create Anyway* and *Adorning the Dark*, respectively. God used your words to spur me on to say yes to this project in the first place and as encouragement again and again in the many unseen, ordinary days of writing.

To Sarah Gillette, Alyssa Trail, Rachel Renzulli, Alyssa Pinkham, Maria Lemoine, and Celeste Santos: Your friendship has, in various ways, made this book and my life better. Thank you.

To my vocational small group: You are, in many ways, the "Inklings" for my own work as a mere Christian. Thank you for challenging me, supporting me, and encouraging me in all my work, including this book.

To Pastors Javin Proctor, Jeff Shipman, and JD Richards: Thank you for seeing and supporting my work. I wish every mere Christian could have pastors like you.

To Brad and Meredith Cox: Thank you for loving me as your own and cheering me on in every new endeavor. Brad, thank you for the endless book recommendations and thoughtful feedback on this work.

To Mom and Dad: "Thank you" feels inadequate. Your unbridled enthusiasm for every single adventure I take has enabled me to write this book and discover my calling.

To Banner: You'll never know what a difference it's made in my life that you've always shown a delighted interest in my work. Thank you for cheering me on. No work has brought me more joy than being your mom.

To Grant: Your support of this project came at a real cost of many hours spent taking care of our home and our son without me. I am forever grateful for your sacrifice. Thank you for being the banks to my river. I love you so much.

To my heavenly Father: Thank you for inviting me to retell these stories you wrote, for all the happy surprises in my own work as a mere Christian thus far, and for always empowering me to do the work to which you call me. It's all for you.

Jordan Raynor is a leading voice of the faith and work movement. Through his bestselling books, podcasts, and devotionals, Jordan has helped millions of Christians throughout the world connect the gospel to their work. In addition to his writing, Jordan serves as the executive chairman of Threshold 360, where he previously served as CEO following a string of his own successful ventures. Jordan has twice been selected as a Google fellow, and he served in the White House under President George W. Bush. A sixth-generation Floridian, Jordan lives in Tampa with his wife and their three young daughters. The Raynors are proud members of The Church at Odessa where Jordan serves as an elder.

Kaleigh Cox is a mere Christian who coauthored this book while working full-time for a marketing startup. A lifelong student of the faith and work movement, Kaleigh now works alongside Jordan Raynor as his vice president of marketing. She is a member of Crossroads Church in Columbia, South Carolina, where she lives with her husband and son.

NOTES

INTRODUCTION

1. Timothy Keller, "The Whirlwind of Jesus," The Apostles' Creed sermon series, January 9, 2000, in *The Timothy Keller Sermon Archive, 1989–2017* (Logos Bible Software edition).

PART I: FRED ROGERS

1. Maxwell King, *The Good Neighbor: The Life and Work of Fred Rogers* (New York: Abrams Press, 2018), 112.

2. Ibid., 123.

3. Jeanne Marie Laskas, "The Mister Rogers No One Saw," *New York Times Magazine*, November 19, 2019, https://www.nytimes.com/2019/11/19/magazine/mr-rogers.html.

4. Amy Hollingsworth, *The Simple Faith of Mister Rogers: Spiritual Insights from the World's Most Beloved Neighbor* (Nashville, TN: Thomas Nelson, 2005), xxviii.

5. This statement is widely attributed to H.L. Mencken, a journalist at *The Baltimore Sun*, but the original source of the statement is unable to be ascertained. One source that confirms the attribution to Mencken is Lynne Olson, *Those Angry Days: Roosevelt, Lindbergh, and America's Fight over World War II, 1939–1941* (New York: Random House, 2014), 10.

6. King, *Good Neighbor*, 30.

7. Hollingsworth, *Simple Faith*, 126.

8. Ibid., 125.

9. Ibid., 124.

10. King, *Good Neighbor*, 37.

11. Ibid., 30.

12. Ibid., 52.

13. Maxwell King, "Maxwell King (Mister Rogers's Biographer)," interviewed by Jordan Raynor, February 18, 2020, in *Mere Christians*, podcast, 44:01, https://podcast.jordanraynor.com/episodes/maxwell-king-mister-rogers-biographer.

14. Ibid.; edited slightly for clarity.

15. Fred Rogers, *The Interviews: An Oral History of Television*, by Karen Herman, Television Academy Foundation, July 22, 1999, https://interviews.televisionacademy.com/interviews/fred-rogers.

16. Ibid.

17. Fred Rogers, commencement speech, Eastern Michigan University, Ypsilanti, MI, April 15, 1973.

18. King, *Good Neighbor*, 44.

19. Shea Tuttle, *Exactly As You Are: The Life and Faith of Mister Rogers* (Grand Rapids, MI: William B. Eerdmans Publishing, 2019), 37.

20. Rogers, *The Interviews*.

21. Ibid.

22. Ibid.

23. Rick Seback, "The Origins of Daniel Striped Tiger," WQED, August 31, 2012, video, 3:57, https://www.youtube.com/watch?v=oqNmv5u4X28.

24. Rogers, *The Interviews*.

25. King, *Good Neighbor*, 110.

26. Josie Carey, *The Interviews: An Oral History of Television*, by Karen Herman, Television Academy Foundation, July 23, 1999, https://interviews.televisionacademy.com/interviews/josie-carey.

27. Ibid.

28. Ibid.

29. King, *Good Neighbor*, 141.

30. Rogers, *The Interviews*.

31. King, *Good Neighbor*, 144.

32. Fred Rogers, "Can You Say...Hero?" interview by Tom Junod, *Esquire*, November 1998 (republished April 6, 2017), https://www.esquire.com/entertainment/tv/a27134/can-you-say-hero-esq1198/.

33. Laskas, "The Mister Rogers No One Saw."

34. Fred Rogers, "Children's TV: What Can the Church Do About It?" reprinted in Tuttle, *Exactly As You Are*, 72.

35. King, *Good Neighbor*, 160.

36. Tuttle, *Exactly As You Are*, 158.

37. Rogers, *The Interviews*.

38. François Clemmons, "StoryCorps 462: In the Neighborhood," interview by Karl Lindholm, *StoryCorps*, podcast, 14:55, March 2016, https://storycorps.org/podcast/storycorps-462-in-the-neighborhood/.

39. *Won't You Be My Neighbor?* directed by Morgan Neville (Universal City, CA: Focus Features, 2018), https://www.youtube.com/watch?v=K6O_Ep9bY0U.

40. Fred Rogers, quoted in Michael G. Long, *Peaceful Neighbor: Discovering the Countercultural Mister Rogers* (Louisville, KY: Westminster John Knox Press, 2015), 2.

41. Hollingsworth, *Simple Faith*, 20.

42. Laskas, "The Mister Rogers No One Saw."

43. Hollingsworth, *Simple Faith*, 36.

44. Tuttle, *Exactly As You Are*, 160.

45. King, *Good Neighbor*, 236.

46. Ibid., 242.

47. "The Messages," Mister Rogers' Neighborhood, accessed February 14, 2024, https://www.misterrogers.org/the-messages/.

48. Hollingsworth, *Simple Faith*, 19.

49. King, *Good Neighbor*, 295.

50. Ibid., 326.

51. "Michael Keaton Gushes About Working on 'Mister Rogers' Neighborhood,'" *ABC News*, October 14, 2014, https://abcnews.go.com/Entertainment/michael-keaton-gushes-working-mister-rogers-neighborhood/story?id=26185850.

52. King, "Maxwell King."

53. Ibid.

54. King, *Good Neighbor*, 312.

55. Andie Judson, "Mr. Rogers Was a Friend to Everyone. But to One Sick Little Girl, He Was a Life Saver," WKYC, December 6, 2018, https://www.wkyc.com/article/syndication/heartthreads/mr-rogers-was-a-friend-to-everyone-but-to-one-sick-little-girl-he-was-a-life-saver/507-621514588.

56. Beth Usher, "How Mister Rogers Saved My Life," *Brain and Life*, August 13, 2018, https://www.brainandlife.org/the-magazine/online-exclusives/speak-uphow-mister-rogers-saved-my-life/.

57. Judson, "Mr. Rogers Was a Friend."

58. Usher, "How Mister Rogers Saved My Life."

59. King, *Good Neighbor*, 302.

60. Tuttle, *Exactly As You Are*, 163.

61. King, *Good Neighbor*, 224.

62. *Mister Rogers' Neighborhood*, season 14, episode 78, "It's You I Like," directed by Fred Rogers, aired February 15, 2010, on PBS, https://www.pbs.org/video/mister-rogers-neighborhood-its-you-i-like/.

63. Academy of Television Arts and Sciences, 14th Annual Hall of Fame, Leonard H. Goldenson Theatre, Los Angeles, February 27, 1999, https://www.youtube.com/watch?v=TcNxY4TudXo.

64. Ibid.

65. Neville, *Won't You Be My Neighbor?*

66. Ibid.

67. "He Talked to Us Honestly About Difficult Subjects," Mister Rogers' Neighborhood, accessed February 14, 2024, https://www.misterrogers.org/articles/he-talked-to-us-honestly-about-difficult-subjects/.

68. Neville, *Won't You Be My Neighbor?*

69. King, *Good Neighbor*, 346.

70. Ibid., 119.

71. Ibid., 349.

72. Neville, *Won't You Be My Neighbor?*

73. Hollingsworth, *Simple Faith*, 20.

74. Charles Spurgeon, "All for Jesus!" (sermon, Metropolitan Tabernacle, London, November 29, 1874), http://www.spurgeongems.org/sermon/chs1205.pdf.

75. Fred Rogers, Latrobe High School baccalaureate speech, Latrobe, PA, June 2, 1996.

76. Hollingsworth, *Simple Faith*, 5.

77. Ibid., 7.

78. King, *Good Neighbor*, 348.

79. Timothy Keller, *The Freedom of Self-Forgetfulness: The Path to True Christian Joy* (Chorley, England: 10Publishing, 2012), 32.

80. King, "Maxwell King."

81. Fred Rogers, speech, Thiel College, Greenville, PA, November 13, 1969.

82. John Mark Comer, *The Ruthless Elimination of Hurry: How to Stay Emotionally Healthy and Spiritually Alive in the Chaos of the Modern World* (Colorado Springs, CO: WaterBrook, 2019), 89.

83. King, *Good Neighbor*, 7.

84. Ibid., 295.

85. Ibid., 9.

PART II: FANNIE LOU HAMER

1. Proceedings of the Democratic National Convention Credentials Committee, Atlantic City, NJ, August 22, 1964, DNC Papers Series 2, Box 102, LBJ Presidential Library, accessed May 16, 2024, https://www.discoverlbj.org/item/pp-dnc-s2-b102-credentialsreport.

2. Ibid.

3. Ibid.

4. "Fanny Lou Hamer Raps in Cincy," *Independent Eye* (Cincinnati), December 23, 1968–January 20, 1969.

5. Jack O'Dell, "Life in Mississippi: An Interview with Fannie Lou Hamer," *Freedomways: A Quarterly Review of the Negro Freedom Movement* 5, no. 2 (Spring 1965): 232.

6. "Fanny Lou Hamer Raps in Cincy."

7. "Fannie Lou Hamer Speaks Out," *Essence*, October 1971, 54.

8. Ibid.

9. Phyl Garland, "Builders of a New South," *Ebony*, August 1966, 29.

10. Howell Raines, *My Soul Is Rested: The Story of the Civil Rights Movement in the Deep South* (New York: Penguin Books, 1983), 255.

11. Fannie Lou Hamer, "Until I Am Free, You Are Not Free Either," in *The Speeches of Fannie Lou Hamer: To Tell It Like It Is*, ed. Maegan Parker Brooks and Davis W. Houck (Jackson: University Press of Mississippi, 2013), 124.

12. Ibid., 106.

13. Ibid.

14. Ibid., xviii.

15. "Right to Vote Not Denied by Race," National Constitution Center, accessed June 25, 2024, https://constitutioncenter.org/the-constitution/amendments/amendment-xv.

16. Michael Newton, *Ku Klux Klan in Mississippi: A History* (Jefferson, NC: McFarland, 2019), 102–4.

17. John Dittmer, *Local People: The Struggle for Civil Rights in Mississippi* (Urbana: University of Illinois Press, 1994), 32–33.

18. "The Trial of J.W. Milam and Roy Bryant," *American Experience*, PBS, accessed February 12, 2024, https://www.pbs.org/wgbh/americanexperience/features/emmett-trial-jw-milam-and-roy-bryant/.

19. Raines, *My Soul Is Rested*, 255.

20. Perry Deane Young, "A Surfeit of Surgery," *Washington Post*, May 30, 1976.

21. Hamer, "Testimony Before a Select Panel on Mississippi and Civil Rights, Washington, D.C., June 8, 1964," in *Speeches of Fannie Lou Hamer*, 40.

22. J. Todd Moye, "Everybody Say Freedom: Using Oral History to Construct and Teach New Civil Rights Narratives," in *Understanding and Teaching the Civil Rights Movement*, ed. Hasan Kwame Jeffries, 197–208 (Madison: University of Wisconsin Press, 2019), 199–200.

23. Charles Marsh, *God's Long Summer: Stories of Faith and Civil Rights* (Princeton: Princeton University Press, 1997), 10–12.

24. Tracy Sugarman, *Stranger at the Gates: A Summer in Mississippi* (Westport, CT: Prospecta Press, 2014), xiii.

25. Raines, *My Soul Is Rested*, 249.

26. Brooks and Houck, "Introduction," in *Speeches of Fannie Lou Hamer*, xix.

27. Fannie Lou Hamer, *To Praise Our Bridges: An Autobiography* (Jackson, MS: KIPCO, 1967), 12, https://snccdigital.org/wp-content/themes/sncc/flipbooks/mev_hamer_updated_2018.

28. Ibid.

29. Sugarman, *Stranger at the Gates*, xiii.

30. Charles McLaurin, "Voice of Calm," *Sojourners*, December 1982, 12.

31. Raines, *My Soul Is Rested*, 250.

32. Hamer, *To Praise Our Bridges*, 13.

33. Raines, *My Soul Is Rested*, 251.

34. Hamer, "I Don't Mind My Light Shining," in *Speeches of Fannie Lou Hamer*, 5.

35. Charles McLaurin, interview by Emilye Crosby, *U.S. Civil Rights History Project*, Library of Congress Archive of Folk Culture, 2015, https://www.youtube.com/watch?v=nb2Nh4RNtJM.

36. Ibid., 90.

37. Ibid., 91.

38. Raines, *My Soul Is Rested*, 253.

39. Kate Clifford Larson, *Walk with Me: A Biography of Fannie Lou Hamer* (New York: Oxford University Press, 2021), 92.

40. Raines, *My Soul Is Rested*, 253.

41. St. John Barrett, *The Drive for Equality: A Personal History of Civil Rights Enforcement, 1954–1965* (Baltimore, MD: PublishAmerica, 2009), 55.

42. Raines, *My Soul Is Rested*, 254.

43. Larson, *Walk with Me*, 101.

44. Keisha N. Blain, "'God Is Not Going to Put It in Your Lap.' What Made Fannie Lou Hamer's Message on Civil Rights So Radical—And So Enduring," *TIME*, October 4, 2019, https://time.com/5692775/fannie-lou-hamer/.

45. Marsh, *God's Long Summer*, 10.

46. Hamer, "We're On Our Way," in *Speeches of Fannie Lou Hamer*, 54.

47. Ibid., 55.

48. Jonathan Eig, *King: A Life* (New York: Farrar, Straus and Giroux, 2023), 440.

49. Hamer, "We're On Our Way," 54.

50. Larson, *Walk with Me*, 121.

51. Ibid.

52. Sally Belfrage, *Freedom Summer* (New York: Viking Press, 1965), 21.

53. Larson, *Walk with Me*, 151.

54. James W. Silver, *Mississippi: The Closed Society*, expanded ed. (New York: Harcourt, Brace & World, 1966), 341.

55. Hamer, "I Don't Mind My Light Shining," *Speeches of Fannie Lou Hamer*, 5.

56. Larry Still, "Shocking Mississippi Testimony Sets Stage for Bitter Dem Fight," *Jet*, September 3, 1964.

57. Stephen Ives, "1964: Interview with Rev. Ed King, Civil Rights Activist, Part 1 of 2," WGBH Educational Foundation, 2014, Video, 59:00, https://video.alexanderstreet.com/watch/1964-interview-with-rev-ed-king-civil-rights-activist-part-1-of-2.

58. Larson, *Walk with Me*, 181.

59. Ives, "1964."

60. Jim Dann, *Challenging Mississippi Firebombers: Memories of Mississippi, 1964–65* (Montreal: Baraka Books, 2013), 119.

61. Larson, *Walk with Me*, 184.

62. Harry Belafonte, *My Song: A Memoir of Art, Race, and Defiance* (New York: Vintage Books, 2011), 293.

63. Henry Hampton and Steve Fayer, *Voices of Freedom: An Oral History of the Civil Rights Movement from the 1950s through the 1980s* (New York: Bantam, 1990), 205.

64. O'Dell, "Life in Mississippi," 241.

65. Hamer, *To Praise Our Bridges*, 23.

66. O'Dell, "Life in Mississippi," 241.

67. Larson, *Walk with Me*, 198.

68. Hamer, "Testimony Before the Subcommittee on Elections of the Committee on House Administration, House of Representatives, Washington, D.C., September 13, 1965," in *Speeches of Fannie Lou Hamer*, 67–68.

69. John Lewis and Michael D'Orso, *Walking with the Wind: A Memoir of the Movement* (New York: Simon & Schuster, 2015), 367.

70. Larson, *Walk with Me*, 218.

71. Ibid., 214.

72. Vergie Hamer Faulkner, interview by Maegan Parker Brooks in *Speeches of Fannie Lou Hamer*, 197.

73. "Mrs. Hamer: Loving and Stalwart," *Delta Democrat-Times* (Greenville, MS), March 21, 1977.

74. Kay Mills, *This Little Light of Mine: The Life of Fannie Lou Hamer* (New York: Dutton, 1993), 309–12.

75. Larson, *Walk with Me*, 3.

76. "Mrs. Hamer: Loving and Stalwart."

77. Larson, *Walk with Me*, 38.

78. Ibid., 60.

79. Larson, *Walk with Me*, 157.

PART III: OLE KIRK CHRISTIANSEN

1. Jens Andersen, *The LEGO Story: How a Little Toy Sparked the World's Imagination* (Boston: Mariner Books, 2022), 56.

2. Ibid., 62.

3. Ibid., 128.

4. Ibid., 25.

5. Ibid.

6. Ibid., 28.

7. Ibid., 33.

8. Ibid., 30.

9. Ibid.

10. Ibid., 38.

11. Ibid., 126.

12. Ibid., 62.

13. Ibid., 81.

14. Ibid., 88.

15. Ibid.

16. Ibid., 154.

17. Ibid., 129.

18. Ibid., 128.

19. Gustavo Gutiérrez, *Job: God-Talk and the Suffering of the Innocent* (Maryknoll, NY: Orbis Books, 1988), 75.

20. Dorothy L. Sayers, "Why Work?" in *Letters to a Diminished Church: Passionate Arguments for the Relevance of Christian Doctrine* (Nashville, TN: Thomas Nelson, 2004), 132.

PART IV: HANNAH MORE

1. Henry Thompson, *The Life of Hannah More, with Notices of Her Sisters* (London: Cadell, 1838), 37–38.

2. Ellen Donkin, *Getting into the Act: Women Playwrights in London, 1776–1829* (London: Routledge, 1995), 60.

3. Ibid., 71.

4. Ibid., 76.

5. Karen Swallow Prior, *Fierce Convictions: The Extraordinary Life of Hannah More; Poet, Reformer, Abolitionist* (Nashville, TN: Nelson Books, 2014), 98.

6. Eric Metaxas, *Seven Men and Seven Women and the Secret of Their Greatness* (Nashville, TN: Nelson Books, 2016), 302.

7. Ibid.

8. Robert Isaac and Samuel Wilberforce, *The Life of William Wilberforce*, 5 vols. (London: John Murray, 1838), 4:358.

9. Metaxas, *Seven Men and Seven Women*, 305.

10. Prior, *Fierce Convictions*, 1.

11. Jean-Jacques Rousseau, *Emile*, trans. and ed. Christopher Kelly and Allan Bloom (Lebanon, NH: University Press of New England, 2009), 540.

12. Prior, *Fierce Convictions*, 18.

13. John Wesley, "The Way to the Kingdom," sermon 7, June 6, 1742, reprinted in Wesley Center Online, http://wesley.nnu.edu/john-wesley/the-sermons-of-john-wesley-1872-edition/sermon-7-the-way-to-the-kingdom/.

14. Quoted in Anne Stott, *Hannah More: The First Victorian* (Oxford: Oxford University Press, 2003), 9–10.

15. Hannah More, *The Search after Happiness: A Pastoral Drama in One Act and in Verse* (Bristol, UK: S. Farley, 1774), 43.

16. Thompson, *The Life of Hannah More*, 14.

17. Jeremy Collingwood and Margaret Collingwood, *Hannah More* (Colorado Springs, CO: Chariot Victor Publishing, 1990), 17.

18. William Roberts, *Memoirs of the Life and Correspondence of Mrs. Hannah More*, 2 vols. (New York: Harper & Brothers, 1834), 1:28.

19. Ibid.

20. Ibid., 1:29.

21. Quoted in Thompson, *Life of Hannah More*, 22.

22. Roberts, *Memoirs*, 1:30.

23. Prior, *Fierce Convictions*, 37.

24. Roberts, *Memoirs*, 1:29; Mary Alden Hopkins, *Hannah More and Her Circle* (London: Longman Green, 1947), 37.

25. Prior, *Fierce Convictions*, 53.

26. Ibid.

27. Stott, *Hannah More*, 25.

28. Thompson, *Life of Hannah More*, 25.

29. Hopkins, *Hannah More*, 62.

30. Collingwood and Collingwood, *Hannah More*, 34.

31. Roberts, *Memoirs*, 1:34.

32. Collingwood and Collingwood, *Hannah More*, 44.

33. Roberts, *Memoirs*, 1:64.

34. Ibid., 1:49.

35. Collingwood and Collingwood, *Hannah More*, 41.

36. Roberts, *Memoirs*, 1:77.

37. Roberts, *Memoirs*, 1:90.

38. Roberts, *Memoirs*, 1:95.

39. Donkin, *Getting into the Act*, 67.

40. John Newton, "Letters to a Nobleman, Letter I," in *Cardiphonia: Letters from a Pastor's Heart* (Aukland, New Zealand: Titus Books, 2013).

41. John Newton, *Amazing Grace*, 1779, https://library .timelesstruths.org/music/Amazing_Grace/.

42. Roberts, *Memoirs*, 1:45.

43. Ibid., 1:46.

44. Newton, "Letters to a Nobleman, Letter XX," in *Cardiphonia*.

45. Newton, "Eight Letters to the Rev. Mr. ——, Letter VIII," in *Cardiphonia*.

46. Collingwood and Collingwood, *Hannah More*, 56.

47. Roberts, *Memoirs*, 1:290.

48. Ibid., 1:291.

49. John S. Harford, *Recollections of William Wilberforce during Nearly Thirty Years* (London: Longman Green, 1864), 216.

50. Metaxas, *Seven Men and Seven Women*, 62.

51. Quoted in M. G. Jones, *Hannah More* (Cambridge: Cambridge University Press, 1952), 91.

52. Roberts, *Memoirs*, 1:286.

53. Isaac and Wilberforce, *Life of William Wilberforce*, 1:149.

54. Roberts, *Memoirs*, 1:266.

55. Isaac and Wilberforce, *Life of William Wilberforce*, 4:112.

56. Hannah More, *Slavery: A Poem*, 1788, https://www .poetryfoundation.org/poems/51885/slavery.

57. Roberts, *Memoirs*, 2:323.

58. Stephen Tomkins, *The Clapham Sect: How Wilberforce's Circle Transformed Britain* (Oxford, UK: Lion Hudson, 2010), 64.

59. Ibid., 12.

60. Hannah More, *Collected Works*, 10 vols. (London: Harrison and Sons, 1853), 1:vii.

61. Martha More, *Mendip Annals or a Narrative of the Charitable Labours of Hannah and Martha More in Their Neighbourhood, Being the Journal of Martha More* (Madrid: HardPress, 2018), 2.

62. Ibid., 17.

63. Ibid.

64. Ibid., 14.

65. Ibid., 15.

66. Ibid., 158.

67. Ibid., 158–59.

68. Ibid., 158.

69. Ibid., 19.

70. Ibid., 23.

71. Ibid., 24.

72. Ibid., 72.

73. Ibid., 36–37.

74. Ibid., 133.

75. Charlotte M. Yonge, *Hannah More* (London: W.H. Allen, 1888), chapter 14.

76. Roberts, *Memoirs*, 2:398.

77. Ibid., 2:428.

78. Ibid.

79. Ibid., 2:448.

80. Ibid., 2:452–53.

81. Ibid., 2:453.

82. Metaxas, *Seven Men and Seven Women*, 293.

83. Stott, *Hannah More*.

84. More, *Collected Works*, 2:275.

85. Kimberly J. Largent, "Harriet Beecher Stowe: The Little Woman Who Wrote the Book that Started This Great War," accessed May 16, 2024, https://ehistory.osu.edu /articles/harriet-beecher-stowe-little-woman-who-wrote -book-started-great-war.

86. Metaxas, *Seven Men and Seven Women*, 305, emphasis added.

87. Eric Metaxas, foreword to Prior, *Fierce Convictions*, xii.

88. Andy Crouch, *Culture Making: Recovering Our Creative Calling* (Downers Grove, IL: InterVarsity Press, 2009), 66.

PART V: C.S. LEWIS

1. Erik Larson, *The Splendid and the Vile: A Saga of Churchill, Family, and Defiance during the Blitz* (New York: Crown, 2020), 179.

2. Ibid., 240.

3. Ibid., 31.

4. Justin Phillips, *C.S. Lewis at the BBC: Messages of Hope in the Darkness of War* (New York: HarperCollins, 2003), 120.

5. Ibid., 119.

6. Alister McGrath, *C.S. Lewis—A Life: Eccentric Genius, Reluctant Prophet* (Carol Stream, IL: Tyndale, 2013), 208.

7. C.S. Lewis, *The Case for Christianity* (Brentwood, TN: B&H Publishing, 2000), 5.

8. McGrath, *C.S. Lewis*, 287.

9. Alan Jacobs, *The Narnian: The Life and Imagination of C.S. Lewis* (New York: PerfectBound, 2005), chapter 1.

10. C.S. Lewis, *Surprised by Joy: The Shape of My Early Life* (San Francisco: HarperOne, 2017), 9.

11. Ibid.

12. C.S. Lewis, *The Lion, the Witch and the Wardrobe*, in *The Chronicles of Narnia: Complete 7-Book Collection* (New York: HarperCollins, 2013), 166.

13. Lewis, *Surprised by Joy*, 4.

14. Ibid., 22.

15. McGrath, *C.S. Lewis*, 24.

16. Douglas Gresham, *Jack's Life: The Life Story of C.S. Lewis* (Brentwood, TN: B&H Books, 2005), 12.

17. Lewis, *Surprised by Joy*, 40.

18. Ibid., 77.

19. Ibid., 75.

20. Ibid., 78.

21. Ibid., 162.

22. Ibid., 162–64.

23. Ibid., 166.

24. Ibid.

25. Ibid.

26. Terry Glaspey, *75 Masterpieces Every Christian Should Know: The Fascinating Stories Behind Great Works of Art, Literature, Music, and Film* (Chicago: Moody, 2021), 177.

27. Lewis, *Surprised by Joy*, 222.

28. Glaspey, *75 Masterpieces*, 177.

29. Harry Lee Poe, *Becoming C.S. Lewis: A Biography of Young Jack Lewis (1898–1918)* (Wheaton, IL: Crossway, 2019), 133.

30. C.S. Lewis, letter to Albert Lewis, December 7, 1916, in *The Collected Letters of C.S. Lewis*, ed. Walter Hooper (San Francisco: HarperOne, 2004), 1:262.

31. Lewis, *Surprised by Joy*, 77.

32. McGrath, *C.S. Lewis*, 61.

33. Poe, *Becoming C.S. Lewis*, 247.

34. Lewis, *Surprised by Joy*, 225.

35. Gresham, *Jack's Life*, 42.

36. Lewis, *Surprised by Joy*, 230–31.

37. Gresham, *Jack's Life*, 47.

38. Quoted in McGrath, *C.S. Lewis*, 85.

39. Harry Lee Poe, *The Making of C.S. Lewis: From Atheist to Apologist (1918–1945)* (Wheaton, IL: Crossway, 2021), 35.

40. McGrath, *C.S. Lewis*, 120.

41. Lewis, *Surprised by Joy*, 275, 279.

42. Ibid., 222.

43. Ibid., 260.

44. Ibid., 261.

45. Ibid., 278.

46. Ibid., 279.

47. McGrath, *C.S. Lewis*, 149–50.

48. Lewis, *Surprised by Joy*, 290.

49. Ibid., 292.

50. A.N. Wilson, "'Tolkien Was Not a Writer,'" *Telegraph* (UK), November 24, 2001, https://www.telegraph.co.uk/culture/4726760/Tolkien-was-not-a-writer.html.

51. McGrath, *C.S. Lewis*, 199.

52. Ibid.

53. Ibid., 240.

54. J.R.R. Tolkien, letter to Joy Hill, May 10, 1966, in *The Letters of J.R.R. Tolkien*, ed. Humphrey Carpenter (London: HarperCollins, 1981), 368–69.

55. McGrath, *C.S. Lewis*, 240.

56. Ibid., 245.

57. Alice von Hildebrand, "C.S. Lewis and Mrs. Moore," Catholic Education Resource Center, accessed April 23, 2024, https://www.catholiceducation.org/en/faith-and-character/faith-and-character/c-s-lewis-and-mrs-moore.html.

58. C.S. Lewis, letter to Arthur Greeves, May 30, 1916, in Hooper, *Collected Letters*, 1:187.

59. C.S. Lewis, "It All Began with a Picture…," Epistle of Dude, November 19, 2018, https://epistleofdude.wordpress.com/2018/11/19/it-all-began-with-a-picture/.

60. McGrath, *C.S. Lewis*, 322.

61. Ibid., 323.

62. C.S. Lewis, letter to Katharine Farrer, October 25, 1956, in Hooper, *Collected Letters*, 3:801.

63. Harry Lee Poe, *The Completion of C.S. Lewis: From War to Joy (1945–1963)* (Wheaton, IL: Crossway, 2022), 295.

64. McGrath, *C.S. Lewis*, 341.

65. Lewis, *Surprised by Joy*, 281.

66. C.S. Lewis, *A Grief Observed* (New York: HarperCollins, 2009), 73.

67. Levi Nunnink, "'Men Must Endure Their Going Hence': The Idea of Death in C.S. Lewis's 'Out of the Silent Planet,'" A Pilgrim in Narnia, July 24, 2018, https://apilgriminnarnia.com/2018/07/24/osp-levi/.

68. McGrath, *C.S. Lewis*, 357.

69. Ibid., 167.

70. Ibid., 363.

71. Aaron Cline Hanbury, "Why C.S. Lewis Never Goes out of Style," *Atlantic*, December 17, 2013, https://www.theatlantic.com/entertainment/archive/2013/12/why-cs-lewis-never-goes-out-of-style/282351/.

72. David S. Dockery, "Books of the Century," *Christianity Today*, April 24, 2000, https://www.christianitytoday.com/ct/2000/april24/5.92.html.

73. McGrath, *C.S. Lewis*, 377.

74. C.S. Lewis, letter to Mary Willis Shelburne, June 28, 1963, in Hooper, *Collected Letters*, 3:1434.

75. C.S. Lewis, *Mere Christianity* (New York: HarperCollins, 1952), 49.

76. C.S. Lewis, letter to Arthur Greeves, October 18, 1931, in Hooper, *Collected Letters*, 1:976.

77. Timothy Keller, *How to Reach the West Again: Six Essential Elements of a Missionary Encounter* (New York: Redeemer City to City, 2020), 18.

78. Timothy Keller, "Tim Keller (Author of *Forgive*)," interview by Jordan Raynor, *Mere Christians*, podcast, 25:58, November 2, 2022, https://podcast.jordanraynor.com/episodes/tim-keller-author-of-forgive.

79. Monique Beals, "The Fastest Growing US Religious Affiliation? 'None,' Poll Says," The Hill, December 14, 2021, https://thehill.com/homenews/state-watch/585764-the-fastest-growing-us-religious-affiliation-none-poll-says.

BIBLIOGRAPHY

PART I: FRED ROGERS

Josie Carey, interview by Karen Herman. *Television Academy Foundation*, July 23, 1999. https://interviews.televisionacademy.com/interviews/josie-carey.

Clemmons, François. "StoryCorps 462: In the Neighborhood." Interview by Karl Lindholm. *StoryCorps*. Podcast, 14:55. March 2016. https://storycorps.org/podcast/storycorps-462-in-the-neighborhood/.

Comer, John Mark. *The Ruthless Elimination of Hurry: How to Stay Emotionally Healthy and Spiritually Alive in the Chaos of the Modern World*. Colorado Springs, CO: WaterBrook, 2019.

Eliot, Marc. *Jimmy Stewart: A Biography*. New York: Random House, 2007.

"Fred Rogers Hall of Fame Induction 1999." Television Academy. Posted November 13, 2017. https://www.emmys.com/video/fred-rogers-hall-fame-induction-1999.

"He Talked to Us Honestly about Difficult Subjects." Mister Rogers' Neighborhood. Accessed February 14, 2024. https://www.misterrogers.org/articles/he-talked-to-us-honestly-about-difficult-subjects/.

Hollingsworth, Amy. *The Simple Faith of Mister Rogers: Spiritual Insights from the World's Most Beloved Neighbor*. Nashville, TN: Thomas Nelson, 2005.

Jenod, Tom. "Can You Say . . . Hero?" *Esquire*, November 1998 (republished April 6, 2017). https://www.esquire.com/entertainment/tv/a27134/can-you-say-hero-esq1198/.

Judson, Andie. "Mr. Rogers Was a Friend to Everyone. But to One Sick Little Girl, He Was a Life Saver." WKYC. December 6, 2018. https://www.wkyc.com/article/syndication/heartthreads/mr-rogers-was-a-friend-to-everyone-but-to-one-sick-little-girl-he-was-a-life-saver/507-621514588.

King, Maxwell. *The Good Neighbor: The Life and Work of Fred Rogers*. New York: Abrams Press, 2018.

———. "Maxwell King (Mister Rogers's Biographer)." Interviewed by Jordan Raynor. *Mere Christians*. February 18, 2020. Podcast, 44:01. https://podcast.jordanraynor.com/episodes/maxwell-king-mister-rogers-biographer.

Laskas, Jeanne Marie. "The Mister Rogers No One Saw." *New York Times Magazine*, November 19, 2019. https://www.nytimes.com/2019/11/19/magazine/mr-rogers.html.

Long, Michael G. *Peaceful Neighbor: Discovering the Countercultural Mister Rogers*. Louisville, KY: Westminster John Knox Press, 2015.

"The Messages." *Mister Rogers' Neighborhood*. Accessed February 14, 2024. https://www.misterrogers.org/the-messages/.

"Michael Keaton Gushes About Working on 'Mister Rogers' Neighborhood.'" *ABC News*, October 14, 2014. https://abcnews.go.com/Entertainment/michael-keaton-gushes-working-mister-rogers-neighborhood/story?id=26185850.

Neville, Morgan, dir. *Won't You Be My Neighbor?* Universal City, CA: Focus Features, 2018.

Rogers, Fred. *The Interviews: An Oral History of Television*, by Karen Herman. Television Academy Foundation, July 22, 1999. https://interviews.televisionacademy.com/interviews/fred-rogers#interview-clips.

———. "Latrobe High School Baccalaureate Speech." Latrobe, PA, June 2, 1996.

———, dir. *Mister Rogers' Neighborhood*. Season 14, episode 78, "It's You I Like." Aired February 15, 2010, on PBS. https://www.pbs.org/video/mister-rogers-neighborhood-its-you-i-like/.

———. Speech at Thiel College, Greenville, PA, November 13, 1969.

Seback, Rick. "The Origins of Daniel Striped Tiger." WQED. August 31, 2012. Video, 3:57. https://www.youtube.com/watch?v=oqNmv5u4X28.

Spurgeon, Charles. "All for Jesus!" Sermon at Metropolitan Tabernacle, London, November 29, 1874. http://www.spurgeongems.org/sermon/chs1205.pdf.

Tuttle, Shea. *Exactly As You Are: The Life and Faith of Mister Rogers*. Grand Rapids, MI: William B. Eerdmans Publishing, 2019.

Usher, Beth. "How Mister Rogers Saved My Life." *Brain and Life*, August 13, 2018. https://www.brainandlife.org/the-magazine/online-exclusives/speak-uphow-mister-rogers-saved-my-life/.

PART II: FANNIE LOU HAMER

Barrett, St. John. *The Drive for Equality: A Personal History of Civil Rights Enforcement, 1954–1965*. Baltimore, MD: PublishAmerica, 2009.

Belafonte, Harry. *My Song: A Memoir of Art, Race, and Defiance*. New York: Vintage Books, 2011.

Belfrage, Sally. *Freedom Summer*. New York: Viking Press, 1965.

Dann, Jim. *Challenging Mississippi Firebombers: Memories of Mississippi, 1964–65*. Montreal: Baraka Books, 2013.

Dittmer, John. *Local People: The Struggle for Civil Rights in Mississippi*. Urbana: University of Illinois Press, 1994.

Eig, Jonathan. *King: A Life*. New York: Farrar, Straus and Giroux, 2023.

"Fannie Lou Hamer Speaks Out." *Essence*, October 1971.

"Fanny Lou Hamer Raps in Cincy." *Independent Eye* (Cincinnati), December 23, 1968–January 20, 1969.

Garland, Phyl. "Builders of a New South." *Ebony*, August 1966.

Hamer, Fannie Lou. *The Speeches of Fannie Lou Hamer: To Tell It Like It Is*. Edited by Maegan Parker Brooks and Davis W. Houck. Jackson: University Press of Mississippi, 2013.

———. *To Praise Our Bridges: An Autobiography.* KIPCO, 1967. https://snccdigital.org/wp-content/themes/sncc/flipbooks/mev_hamer_updated_2018.

Hampton, Henry, and Steve Fayer. *Voices of Freedom: An Oral History of the Civil Rights Movement from the 1950s through the 1980s.* New York: Bantam, 1990.

Ives, Stephen. "1964: Interview with Rev. Ed King, Civil Rights Activist, Part 1 of 2." WGBH Educational Foundation, 2014. Video, 59:00. https://video.alexanderstreet.com/watch/1964-interview-with-rev-ed-king-civil-rights-activist-part-1-of-2.

Larson, Kate Clifford. *Walk with Me: A Biography of Fannie Lou Hamer.* New York: Oxford University Press, 2021.

Lewis, John, and Michael D'Orso. *Walking with the Wind: A Memoir of the Movement.* New York: Simon & Schuster, 2015.

Marsh, Charles. *God's Long Summer: Stories of Faith and Civil Rights.* Princeton: Princeton University Press, 1997.

McLaurin, Charles. *U.S. Civil Rights History Project.* Interview by Emilye Crosby. Library of Congress Archive of Folk Culture, 2015. https://www.youtube.com/watch?v=nb2Nh4RNtJM.

———. "Voice of Calm." *Sojourners*, December 1982.

Mills, Kay. *This Little Light of Mine: The Life of Fannie Lou Hamer.* New York: Dutton, 1993.

Moye, J. Todd. "Everybody Say Freedom: Using Oral History to Construct and Teach New Civil Rights Narratives." In *Understanding and Teaching the Civil Rights Movement*, edited by Hasan Kwame Jeffries, 197–208. Madison: University of Wisconsin Press, 2019.

"Mrs. Hamer: Loving and Stalwart." *Delta Democrat-Times* (Greenville, MS), March 21, 1977.

Newton, Michael. *Ku Klux Klan in Mississippi: A History.* Jefferson, NC: McFarland, 2019.

O'Dell, Jack. "Life in Mississippi: An Interview with Fannie Lou Hamer." *Freedomways: A Quarterly Review of the Negro Freedom Movement* 5, no. 2 (Spring 1965): 231–42.

Raines, Howell. *My Soul Is Rested: The Story of the Civil Rights Movement in the Deep South.* New York: Penguin Books, 1983.

Silver, James W. *Mississippi: The Closed Society.* New York: Harcourt, Brace & World, 1966.

"The State of Mississippi in 1964." *American Experience.* PBS, 2014. Video, 2:57. https://www.pbs.org/wgbh/americanexperience/features/freedomsummer-mississippi-1964/.

Still, Larry. "Shocking Mississippi Testimony Sets Stage for Bitter Dem Fight." *Jet*, September 3, 1964.

Sugarman, Tracy. *Stranger at the Gates: A Summer in Mississippi.* Westport, CT: Prospecta Press, 2014.

"The Trial of J.W. Milam and Roy Bryant." *American Experience.* PBS. Accessed February 12, 2024. https://www.pbs.org/wgbh/americanexperience/features/emmett-trial-jw-milam-and-roy-bryant/.

Young, Perry Deane. "A Surfeit of Surgery." *Washington Post*, May 30, 1976.

PART III: OLE KIRK CHRISTIANSEN

Andersen, Jens. *The LEGO Story: How a Little Toy Sparked the World's Imagination.* Boston: Mariner Books, 2022.

"The Beginning of the LEGO Group." LEGO History. Accessed May 16, 2024. http://www.lego.com/en-sg/history/articles/b-the-beginning-of-the-lego-group.

"Disaster Strikes." LEGO History. Accessed May 16, 2024. http://www.lego.com/en-sg/history/articles/c-disaster-strikes.

Ericsson, Anders, and Robert Pool. *Peak: Secrets from the New Science of Expertise.* Boston: Houghton Mifflin Harcourt, 2016.

Gutiérrez, Gustavo. *Job: God-Talk and the Suffering of the Innocent.* Maryknoll, NY: Orbis Books, 1988.

Herman, Sarah. *A Million Little Bricks: The Unofficial Illustrated History of the LEGO Phenomenon.* New York: Skyhorse, 2012.

"Kristiansen or Christiansen." LEGO History. Accessed May 16, 2024. http://www.lego.com/en-sg/history/articles/a-kristiansen-or-christiansen.

"A New Reality." LEGO History. Accessed May 16, 2024. http://www.lego.com/en-sg/history/articles/a-new-reality.

"Ole Kirk Kristiansen's Childhood and Youth." LEGO History. Accessed May 16, 2024. http://www.lego.com/en-sg/history/articles/ole-kirk-kristiansen-s-childhood-and-youth.

"Ole Kirk Kristiansen Settles in Billund." LEGO History. Accessed May 16, 2024. http://www.lego.com/en-sg/history/articles/ole-kirk-kristiansen-settles-in-billund.

Perman, Matthew. *What's Best Next: How the Gospel Transforms the Way You Get Things Done.* Grand Rapids, MI: Zondervan, 2016.

Sayers, Dorothy. "Why Work?" In *Letters to a Diminished Church: Passionate Arguments for the Relevance of Christian Doctrine.* Nashville, TN: Thomas Nelson, 2004.

PART IV: HANNAH MORE

Abramovitch, Seth. "Joe Biden Cites 'Will & Grace' in Endorsement of Same-Sex Marriage (Video)." *Hollywood Reporter*, May 6, 2012. https://www.hollywoodreporter.com/tv/tv-news/joe-biden-cites-will-grace-320724-0-320724/.

"Clapham Sect." Wikipedia. Accessed April 23, 2024. https://en.wikipedia.org/wiki/Clapham_Sect.

Collingwood, Jeremy, and Margaret Collingwood. *Hannah More.* Colorado Springs, CO: Chariot Victor Publishing, 1990.

Crossley-Evans, Martin J. *Hannah More.* Bristol, UK: Bristol Branch of the Historical Association, 1999.

Crouch, Andy. *Culture Making: Recovering Our Creative Calling.* Downers Grove, IL: InterVarsity Press, 2009.

Donkin, Ellen. *Getting into the Act: Women Playwrights in London, 1776–1829.* London: Routledge, 1995.

Harford, John S. *Recollections of William Wilberforce during Nearly Thirty Years.* London: Longman Green, 1864.

Hopkins, Mary Alden. *Hannah More and Her Circle.* London: Longman Green, 1947.

Irving, Echo. "A Brief Life of Hannah More." Wrington, 2007. https://wringtonsomerset.org.uk/morelocke/irvingonmore.html.

Isaac, Robert Isaac, and Samuel Wilberforce. *The Life of William Wilberforce.* 5 vols. London: John Murray, 1838.

Jones, M.G. *Hannah More.* Cambridge: Cambridge University Press, 1952.

Largent, Kimberly J. "Harriet Beecher Stowe: The Little Woman Who Wrote the Book That Started This Great War." Accessed May 16, 2024. https://ehistory.osu.edu/articles/harriet-beecher-stowe-little-woman-who-wrote-book-started-great-war.

Metaxas, Eric. *Seven Men and Seven Women and the Secret of Their Greatness.* Nashville, TN: Nelson Books, 2016.

More, Hannah. *Collected Works.* 10 vols. London: Harrison and Sons, 1853.

———. *The Search after Happiness: A Pastoral Drama in One Act and in Verse.* Bristol, UK: S. Farley, 1774.

———. *Slavery: A Poem.* 1788. https://www.poetryfoundation.org/poems/51885/slavery.

More, Martha. *Mendip Annals or a Narrative of the Charitable Labours of Hannah and Martha More in Their Neighbourhood, Being the Journal of Martha More.* Madrid: HardPress, 2018.

Newton, John. *Cardiphonia: Letters from a Pastor's Heart.* Aukland, New Zealand: Titus Books, 2013.

Prior, Karen Swallow. *Fierce Convictions: The Extraordinary Life of Hannah More: Poet, Reformer, Abolitionist.* Nashville, TN: Nelson Books, 2014.

Roberts, William. *Memoirs of the Life and Correspondence of Mrs. Hannah More.* 2 vols. New York: Harper & Brothers, 1834.

Rousseau, Jean-Jacques. *Emile.* Translated and edited by Christopher Kelly and Allan Bloom. Lebanon, NH: University Press of New England, 2009.

Stott, Anne. *Hannah More: The First Victorian.* Oxford: Oxford University Press, 2003.

Thompson, Henry. *The Life of Hannah More, with Notices of Her Sisters.* London: Cadell, 1838.

Tomkins, Stephen. *The Clapham Sect: How Wilberforce's Circle Transformed Britain.* Oxford, UK: Lion Hudson, 2010.

Wesley, John. "The Way to the Kingdom." Sermon 7, June 6, 1742. Reprinted in Wesley Center Online. *http://wesley.*nnu.edu/john-wesley/the-sermons-of-john-wesley-1872-edition/sermon-7-the-way-to-the-kingdom/.

Yonge, Charlotte M. *Hannah More.* London: W.H. Allen, 1888.

PART V: C.S. LEWIS

Beals, Monique. "The Fastest Growing US Religious Affiliation? 'None,' Poll Says." *The Hill*, December 14, 2021. https://thehill.com/homenews/state-watch/585764-the-fastest-growing-us-religious-affiliation-none-poll-says.

Dockery, David S. "Books of the Century." *Christianity Today*, April 24, 2000. https://www.christianitytoday.com/ct/2000/april24/5.92.html.

Glaspey, Terry. *75 Masterpieces Every Christian Should Know: The Fascinating Stories Behind Great Works of Art, Literature, Music, and Film.* Chicago: Moody, 2021.

Green, Michael. *Evangelism in the Early Church.* Rev. ed. Grand Rapids, MI: Eerdmans, 2003.

Gresham, Douglas. *Jack's Life: The Life Story of C.S. Lewis.* Brentwood, TN: B&H Books, 2005.

Hanbury, Aaron Cline. "Why C.S. Lewis Never Goes Out of Style." *Atlantic*, December 17, 2013. https://www.theatlantic.com/entertainment/archive/2013/12/why-cs-lewis-never-goes-out-of-style/282351/.

Jacobs, Alan. *The Narnian: The Life and Imagination of C.S. Lewis.* New York: PerfectBound, 2005.

Keller, Timothy. *How to Reach the West Again: Six Essential Elements of a Missionary Encounter.* New York: Redeemer City to City, 2020.

———. "Tim Keller (Author of *Forgive*)," interview by Jordan Raynor. *Mere Christians*. November 2, 2022. Podcast, 25:58. https://podcast.jordanraynor.com/episodes/tim-keller-author-of-forgive.

Larson, Erik. *The Splendid and the Vile: A Saga of Churchill, Family, and Defiance During the Blitz.* New York: Crown, 2020.

Lewis, C.S. *The Case for Christianity.* Brentwood, TN: B&H Publishing, 2000.

———. *The Collected Letters of C.S. Lewis (Volume 1).* Edited by Walter Hooper. San Francisco: HarperOne, 2004.

———. *The Collected Letters of C.S. Lewis (Volume 3).* Edited by Walter Hooper. San Francisco: HarperOne, 2004.

———. *A Grief Observed.* New York: HarperCollins, 2009.

———. "It All Began with a Picture . . ." November 19, 2018. https://epistleofdude.wordpress.com/2018/11/19/it-all-began-with-a-picture/.

———. *The Lion, the Witch and the Wardrobe.* In *The Chronicles of Narnia: Complete 7-Book Collection*, 161–293. New York: HarperCollins, 2013.

———. *Mere Christianity.* New York: HarperCollins, 1952.

———. *Surprised by Joy: The Shape of My Early Life.* San Francisco: HarperOne, 2017.

Marsden, George. "Mere Christianity: A Reader's Guide to the Christian Classic." *Desiring God*, July 30, 2021. https://www.desiringgod.org/articles/mere-christianity.

McGrath, Alister. *C.S. Lewis—A Life: Eccentric Genius. Reluctant Prophet.* Carol Stream, IL: Tyndale, 2013.

Nunnink, Levi. "'Men Must Endure Their Going Hence': The Idea of Death in C.S. Lewis's 'Out of the Silent Planet.'" July 24, 2018. https://apilgriminnarnia.com/2018/07/24/osp-levi/.

Phillips, Justin. *C.S. Lewis at the BBC: Messages of Hope in the Darkness of War.* New York: HarperCollins, 2003.

Poe, Harry Lee. *Becoming C.S. Lewis: A Biography of Young Jack Lewis (1898–1918).* Wheaton, IL: Crossway, 2019.

———. *The Completion of C.S. Lewis: From War to Joy (1945–1963).* Wheaton, IL: Crossway, 2022.

———. *The Making of C.S. Lewis: From Atheist to Apologist (1918–1945).* Wheaton, IL: Crossway, 2021.

Tolkien, J.R.R. *The Letters of J.R.R. Tolkien.* Edited by Humphrey Carpenter. London: HarperCollins, 1981.

von Hildebrand, Alice. "C.S. Lewis and Mrs. Moore." Catholic Education Resource Center. Accessed April 23, 2024. https://www.catholiceducation.org/en/faith-and-character/faith-and-character/c-s-lewis-and-mrs-moore.html.

Wilson, A.N. "'Tolkien Was Not a Writer.'" *Telegraph* (UK), November 24, 2001. https://www.telegraph.co.uk/culture/4726760/Tolkien-was-not-a-writer.html.